The **Essential** Buyer's Guide

TRIUMPH
TR7 & TR8

All models (including Sprint & Spider variants)
1975 to 1982

Your marque expert: Roger Williams

VELOCE PUBLISHING
THE PUBLISHER OF FINE AUTOMOTIVE BOOKS

Also from Veloce –

Veloce's Essential Buyer's Guide Series
Alfa GT (Booker)
Alfa Romeo Spider Giulia (Booker & Talbott)
Austin Seven (Barker)
BMW GS (Henshaw)
BSA Bantam (Henshaw)
BSA 500 & 650 Twins (Henshaw)
Citroën 2CV (Paxton)
Citroën ID & DS (Heilig)
Corvette C2 1963-1967 (Falconer)
Fiat 500 & 600 (Bobbitt)
Ford Capri (Paxton)
Harley-Davidson Big Twins (Henshaw)
Hinckley Triumph triples & fours 750, 900, 955,
    1000, 1050, 1200 – 1991-2009 (Henshaw)
Honda CBR600 (Henshaw)
Honda FireBlade (Henshaw)
Honda SOHC fours 1969-1984 (Henshaw)
Jaguar E-type 3.8 & 4.2-litre (Crespin)
Jaguar E-type V12 5.3-litre (Crespin)
Jaguar XJ 1995-2003 (Crespin)
Jaguar/Daimler XJ6, XJ12 & Sovereign (Crespin)
Jaguar/Daimler XJ40 (Crespin)
Jaguar XJ-S (Crespin)
Land Rover Series I, II & IIA (Thurman)
MGB & MGB GT (Williams)
Mercedes-Benz 280SL-560DSL Roadsters (Bass)
Mercedes-Benz 'Pagoda' 230SL, 250SL & 280SL
    Roadsters & Coupés (Bass)
MG Midget & A-H Sprite (Horler)
MG TD, TF & TF1500 (Jones)
Mini (Paxton)
Morris Minor & 1000 (Newell)
Norton Commando (Henshaw)
Peugeot 205 GTi (Blackburn)
Porsche 911 (964) (Streather)
Porsche 911 (993) (Streather)
Porsche 911 (996) (Streather)
Porsche 911 SC (Streather)
Porsche 928 (Hemmings)
Rolls-Royce Silver Shadow & Bentley T-Series
    (Bobbitt)
Subaru Impreza (Hobbs)
Triumph Bonneville (Henshaw)
Triumph Spitfire & GT6

Triumph Stag (Mort & Fox)
Triumph TR6 (Williams)
Triumph TR7 & TR8 (Williams)
Vespa Scooters – Classic 2-stroke models
    1960-2008 (Paxton)
VW Beetle (Cservenka & Copping)
VW Bus (Cservenka & Copping)
VW Golf GTI (Cservenka & Copping)

From Veloce Publishing's new imprints:

BATTLE CRY!

Soviet General & field rank officer uniforms: 1955 to
    1991 (Streather)
Soviet military and paramilitary services: female
    uniforms 1941-1991 (Streather)

Hubble & Hattie

Complete Dog Massage Manual, The – Gentle Dog
    Care (Robertson)
Dinner with Rover (Paton-Ayre)
Dog Cookies (Schops)
Dog Games – Stimulating play to entertain your dog
    and you (Blenski)
Dog Relax – Relaxed dogs, relaxed owners (Pilguj)
Excercising your puppy: a gentle & natural approach
    (Robertson)
Know Your Dog – The guide to a beautiful
    relationship (Birmelin)
Living with an Older Dog (Alderton & Hall)
My dog is blind – but lives life to the full! (Horsky)
Smellorama – nose games for dogs (Theby)
Swim to Recovery: The Animal Magic Way (Wong)
Waggy Tails & Wheelchairs (Epp)
Winston ... the dog who changed my life (Klute)
You and Your Border Terrier – The Essential Guide
    (Alderton)
You and Your Cockapoo – The Essential Guide
    (Alderton)

www.veloce.co.uk

First published in August 2010 by Veloce Publishing Limited, Veloce House, Parkway Farm Business Park,
Middle Farm Way, Poundbury, Dorchester, Dorset, DT1 3AR, England. Fax 01305 250479/
e-mail info@veloce.co.uk/web www.veloce.co.uk or www.velocebooks.com.

ISBN: 978-1-845843-16-8 UPC: 6-36847-04316-2

British Library Cataloguing in Publication Data – A catalogue record for this book is available from the British
Library. Typesetting, design and page make-up all by Veloce Publishing Ltd on Apple Mac.
Printed in India by Imprint Digital.

The purpose of this book is to offer a quick step-by-step guide to finding a 1998cc Drop-head Convertible (DHC) or Fixed-head Coupe (FHC) TR7, TR7-V8 conversion, or TR8, matched to your budget and ambitions. The task is not as easy as it first sounds, if only because owners' descriptions are, all too often, over-optimistic, and some cars have lots of problems hidden under their seductive exteriors. We therefore need to sort the wheat from the chaff.

A superb example of a TR7 Drop-head Convertible.

Whatever the standard of car you seek, it will be out there, and finding it and helping you pay a fair price for it is the primary objective of this book. However, you need to start by making two decisions, the first of which is what are you prepared to pay. Clearly, it is pointless looking at ◑ x4000 cars with ◑ x2000 available. Take care, however, for you need to crosscheck prices carefully from the various magazines and by looking at several cars to ensure you have not set yourself an impossible task with basically inadequate funds.

A good TR7, but in the less popular and consequently less expensive Fixed-head Coupe bodystyle.

The UK magazine *Classic & Sports Car* carries a monthly valuation review under the headings of Show, Average, and Restoration. The magazine also offers a good on-line valuation and, consequently, is probably your best cost reference, but *Practical Classics* also offers an in-magazine price guide under Good, Average, and Rough. While you would be wise to take these periodicals into account, all need to be used *very* carefully; for at best they give an average figure for each category, and individual interpretations and valuations can vary by wide margins. Today, most readers will have the advantage of broadband internet services and a few minutes' surfing should provide numerous price comparisons from trade and private vendors.

Although genuine TR8 DHCs are relatively rare, this is an excellent V8 conversion; almost indistinguishable from the factory originals but available at a fraction of the price.

However, nothing beats seeing cars, asking questions, and getting the feel of the market. Many vendors may rate you as a 'time waster' if you give their car a 15-minute once-over without buying, but it is essential you view a number of cars that seem to fall into your price and condition target before actually getting your wedge (pun intended) out of the bank! If you think you like what you see, you can always take a few pictures and return to carry out a serious evaluation at a later date.

Along with the price issue is the related question as to whether you are buying privately or from a dealer. So, what is your safety net position? Put another way, how much redress do you want? This can only be assessed by each individual and

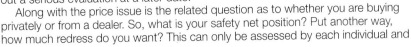

many will be happy to pay perhaps 20% more to a reputable dealer comfortable in the knowledge that if anything goes wrong they should be able to pick up the phone and get help. Buying from a private vendor may save you some money but there is little redress and you are best advised to take this route only if you have good technical knowledge or the close support of someone who 'knows his onions.' Even so, you need your 'buyer-beware' hat on when viewing dealers' cars, and to get the warranty terms clearly specified, before you purchase.

Particularly if going the 'private' route, be prepared to travel long distances and still be disappointed. There will be several frustrating trips where you feel the vendor was wasting your time, but the right car is out there and will make it all worthwhile when you find it, so be patient and persistent.

Whether the task is made easier or more difficult by the TR7's initial shortcomings is debatable. Many cars will have hand brake or gearbox upgrades, for example, which makes like-for-like comparisons difficult. Two 1998cc models were available, with the vast majority of components being interchangeable. Extraordinarily, with hindsight, the Coupe was produced for all seven years of the car's life (1975 to 1981 inclusive), but the Drop-head variant – which has proved much the more popular and sought-after model – was produced for only half that time (more detail in

A 1981 Sprint Drop-head Convertible. Doubtless a very professional and attractive conversion because those few original factory cars that 'escaped' were all Fixed-head Coupes.

Chapter 17). Consequently, the Coupe offers a particularly low-cost route into classic car motoring and, as such, should not be overlooked by first-time classic buyers.

There were significant changes in specification during production, as well as, in turn, three manufacturing locations. A major improvement was made to the gearbox and rear axle with the introduction of the 5-speed models, initially for the US but later for the UK market. The engine was not overlooked either: a much-improved TR7 four-cylinder 'Sprint' variant was tried, while the highly desirable V8 'TR8'

finally came into being, mainly for the US market. Sadly, both these upgraded engine models were made in very small numbers in the context of automotive production, although numerous TR7 conversions have since taken place. Nevertheless, in spite of all the things running against the TR7 range, a commendable total of over 112,000 vehicles were built.

Thanks

I am indebted to Brad Wilson (Wedgeparts) and Richard Connew (World Wide TR7 TR8 Owners) for their help, guidance, many valuable suggestions, and photographic contributions to the preparation of this book. Gary Fuqua (Classic Sports Cars Inc), Tim Lanocha (Lanocha Racing Inc), Steve Taylor, Wayne Walsh, and Pete Whitehorn also contributed valuable photographs, for which I sincerely thank them, too. I would also record my appreciation for the help British Motor Heritage Ltd gave in the preparation of Chapter 17. Without all these contributors this book would have remained still-born. Thanks also goes to Heather Hayes for the cover photograph.

Contents

Essential Buyer's Guide™ currency

At the time of publication a BG unit of currency " ◉ " equals approximately £1.00/ US$2.00/Euro 1.10. Please adjust to suit current exchange rates.

1 Is it the right car for you?
– marriage guidance

Tall and short drivers

Standard seat adjustment is good and will accommodate virtually all drivers. Access is good, although the side sills/rockers are deep.

The pedals are nicely placed.

There is an abundance of legroom.

Currently untrimmed, this shows the 'shelf' behind the seats to good effect. The stowed hood uses the space in the DHC, but it is available as extra luggage capacity in FHC models.

Controls

The steering, gear lever, and pedals are easy to use, but by modern standards the brakes in standard/stock condition are very poor. The gear change on the early four-speed gearboxes is usually smooth unless the gearbox is worn. It can be 'notchy' on the later and much preferable 5-speed gearboxes, but usually only when cold. Handling is predictable and easy to control.

Will it fit the garage?

Length	4.06m/160in
Width	1.58m/62in
Height (Coupe)	1.27m/50in

Interior space

The cabin interior is spacious with excellent head and leg-room. In particular, the distance between the steering wheel and driver's legs is generous compared with many sports cars.

The use of soft bags is recommended, particularly with a TR8 or TR7 V8 conversion when the battery will be relocated to, and occupy some luggage space in, the boot/trunk. This picture shows the rare repatriated Spider variant (detailed later in the book).

Luggage capacity

The available boot/trunk space in a standard TR7 is reasonable. There is some extra capacity on a rear cockpit shelf in the Coupe models, but the seats will not fold forward to allow easy access.

Running costs

The owners/workshop manual provides a comprehensive list of maintenance tasks at 3000, 6000, and 12,000 miles (5000, 10,000, and 20,000km) most of which are simple DIY tasks. However, the 12,000-mile EGR valve, air-conditioning, and air-injection (anti-pollution) checks on US cars may best be carried out by professionals with the appropriate equipment. The cooling system is best flushed through every 12 months and new anti-freeze with the appropriate anti-corrosion additives used. If the car is used as a daily-driver, the engine oil/filter

The EGR (exhaust gas re-circulating)-valve is part of the engine's emission control equipment, and is fitted to reduce peak combustion temperatures, thus reducing harmful emissions.

needs changing every 3000 miles, regardless of what the books say (in the interests of minimising timing chain wear), while if little used, change both every 12 months.

Usability
Today, the Drop-head is a fun/second car, rather than a daily-driver for most owners, although a well-maintained Coupe could be used on a daily basis. Cars still fitted with the 4-speed gearbox and associated banjo rear-axle, in particular, are definitely second/collectors cars.

Parts availability
Good. Numerous specialist suppliers on both sides of the Atlantic provide a fairly comprehensive new parts service from stock, although some of the mechanical parts and trims are no longer available. There are many used spares available.

Parts costs
Generally very good. See Chapter 2 for a more detailed list of new parts costs.

Insurance
Costs can be quite modest if arranged through a recognised club scheme by an older driver with an exemplary record, but many factors affect the final cost.

Investment potential
Poor. The rising cost of restorations, particularly bodyshell and re-painting, coupled with softening resale prices over the last three years, make it difficult for most owners to recover all their purchase and subsequent restoration costs. Better to buy a well-restored car at a fair price.

Foibles
Several – see Chapter 3.

Plus points
Great eye-catching top-down motoring in a Drop-head, with real performance potential from Sprint and V8 versions, particularly tuned examples.

Minus points
The youngest TR7 will be over 30 years old by the time you read these words, so there are inevitably going to be unexpected problems, irritations and repair bills.

Alternatives
To TR7 Drop-head: Triumph Spitfire, TR4, '4A or '6, Alfa-Romeo Spider, Mazda MX5
To TR8: MGB V8 Costello conversion, TVR Griffith
To TR7 Fixed-head Coupe: Triumph GT6, VW Scirocco, Toyota Celica, Porsche 924

2 Cost considerations
– affordable, or a money pit?

Prices exclude taxes:

TR7 new mechanical parts

3-piece clutch set	●x100
Clutch master cylinder	●x45
Clutch slave cylinder	●x43
Front brake discs (standard, each)	●x15
Uprated front discs (each)	●x110
Front brake pads (Kevlar)	●x23
Rear brake shoes (set)	●x10
Rear slave cylinder (each)	●x11
Exhaust (excl manifold)	●x125
Stainless manifold (RHD)	●x152
Radiator (uprated 4-core exchange)	●x165

Mild steel exhaust systems all rust from the inside as well as the outside, so it makes sense to pay extra for the longevity of a stainless steel system.

The distributor is key to reliability so, when wear is evident, buy a service-exchange unit. This is one of the many V8 distributor variants.

Set of water hoses	●x30
Alternator (exchange)	●x72
Distributor (exchange)	●x132
Front shock absorbers (inserts, each)	●x50
Uprated brake servo/master cylinder assembly	●x185
Cylinder head gasket	●x11

The 5-speed gearbox seen here is much the more robust of the two gearboxes fitted to the TR7.

The diaphragm clutch pressure plate – but be sure to fit a three-piece set when required.

Cylinder head (exchange) x375
Gearbox/trans rebuild x480
Rear axle rebuild x430
Propeller shaft (new) x95
Fuel tank (new) x165
Fuel pump (mechanical) x24
Carburettors (pair, service exchange) x255
Alloy wheels (each) x85

Body parts, new unless stated otherwise
Complete body panel restoration kit x925
Front wings/fenders (each) x175
Rear wings/fenders (each) x230
Sill/rocker per side x140
Bonnet/hood x150
Door x315
Door skin x46
Boot/trunk lid x175
Windscreen/windshield x103
Complete internal trim kit (panels, seats, carpets) x1000
New leather-covered seats x536
New hood cover – vinyl x216
Pair of used rear light clusters (new, nla) x100

Most US new parts emanate from the UK, consequently the above figures have a bearing on costs in the US adjusted by currency exchanges at the time of purchase.

– will you get along together?

The engine, thanks to its 45-degree slant, sits nicely in the TR7's engine bay in spite of the unusually low bonnet/hood-line.

The Sprint variants, original or conversions, are easily distinguished ...

... as are the V8 models.

One of the attractions of the TR7 family is that they are several cars – notably the open Drop-head Convertible (DHC) and the enclosed Fixed-head Coupe (FHC) with, in original form, the standard 1998cc engine, Sprint 16-valve 2000cc, and the 3528cc V8 engine options. US drivers, lucky them, also have the benefit of some models fitted with electronic fuel-injection, and the Spider, too, the latter only available in black with red reflective exterior markings. The Sprint and V8 versions are so attractive that businesses have sprung up in the UK supplying specific parts for them, and/or carrying out conversions. The original V8-engined car was called TR8 and to my mind is the model's pinnacle, although it was introduced too late in the production-run and only 20 original cars were made with right hand drive, the other 2770 were exported to the US. So the conversion industry is good news, and I welcome it improving the original TR7, however, it does mean that potential purchasers of these variants need to be aware that the 'original' car they are going to look at may in fact be a conversion and, although an excellent car, possibly overpriced. There are ways to check, which we will outline later in the book.

Both the Drop-head (convertible) and Coupe are great fun to drive courtesy of the excellent rack and pinion steering, but the standard TR7's 105bhp (92bhp in US versions) is very modest compared to modern sports cars, and, consequently, they cannot be classed as a high performance car these days. In fact, acceleration would be termed ponderous (0-60mph, 9.1sec) and the car is unlikely to out-perform many a modern hatchback. However, they are far more distinctive than the modern hatchbacks, besides which there are the more exciting variants to consider. The original Sprint, although few and far between, provided 127bhp, while the original TR8 generated (it must be said, a very modest) 135bhp; but with effortless torque and is easily upgraded such that many provide 175-190bhp while still with 3500cc, generating the excellent performance that goes with such power. For its day, the suspension design was very good but overly soft for sporty use, purely because the car was conceived as a US straight-line cruiser. Consequently, many cars have since enjoyed a suspension upgrade comprising harder bushes and road springs.

The brakes were also designed for US road-conditions, with a 55mph speed restriction in mind, and were never up to the car's reputed 110mph top speed, despite a servo being fitted as standard to all cars. Consequently, there are numerous upgrade ideas and several kits available. Although this very desirable improvement is not entirely straightforward, requiring both calliper and servo/master cylinder changes (and in my opinion larger diameter road wheels), so prospective purchases need to be checked out with care – perhaps by a professional.

You would be wise to enquire, certainly before undertaking a long journey, that a potential purchase's gearbox meets your expectations. A number of automatic cars were produced and some are still offered for sale, while the early TR7's, sold in both the UK and US, were fitted not only with a weak 4-speed gearbox but a fragile 'banjo'-constructed 3.63 ratio rear axle. This gearbox lacks the all-important 5th or overdrive/high-ratio gear so necessary for today's motorway, Auto-route, or Interstate journeys. The introduction of stronger Rover-based designs, via a 5-speed gearbox and 3.9:1 (or lower) ratio rear axle, solved this issue and provided immeasurable improvements. You would have to be constrained by originality issues to select a car with a 4-speed gearbox. In fact most 4-speed TR7s have been retrospectively upgraded to employ the later components, but you should check before setting off to view, and check if applicable that the upgrade has been well carried out.

The TR7's electrical systems also need careful examination generally. However, the headlight lift/lower mechanism and dashboard/fascia switches are particularly prone to unreliability, both usually caused by dirty connections. A shop window (or friend) will help check the consistency of the headlight operation, and a relay dominated electrical upgrade with evidence of high-quality earth/ground returns will reduce the current flowing through the car's cheap original switches.

So, there are several 'buyer-beware' issues if you are going to live happily with a TR7 or its variants. If you are seeking an original car with Concours competitions in mind, you are obliged to seek a late (Solihull-produced) original 5-speed car for its general build quality. No TR7 was built to last 30 or so years, even the Solihull models, but the earlier Speke and Canley units were, respectively, of very and slightly dubious build quality, and the speed and extent of the corrosion in all bodyshells reflect these sad facts. Thus, most buyers will be searching for an impeccably restored bodyshell that was well painted and thoroughly rustproofed at the time, and you will find that Chapters 7 and 9 reflect this.

Finally, any old car is probably not best suited to owners unwilling to get their hands dirty from time to time, although I know several owners who know little about cars generally and get along with their '7s in perfect harmony with the aid of interested local garages/specialists.

4 Relative values
– which model for you?

There is more detail on values in Chapter 12, but this chapter expresses, in percentages, the relative value of the individual models in the UK.

Four-cylinder models
TR7 Drop-head 100%
TR7 Coupe 50-60%
TR7 Sprint (original), FHC 120-130%
TR7 FHC Sprint conversion 60-80%
TR7 Drop-head Sprint conversion 90-110%

A repatriated TR7 Efi car. The engine bay makes an interesting comparison with the more usual carburettor car in the previous chapter.

Another 16-valve Sprint conversion, this time Steve Taylor's significantly tuned car with body kit and MGF 16in wheels, to accommodate the larger diameter brake discs he wisely fitted.

Notes
There are a number of repatriated warm climate cars that come onto the UK market each year. Many remain in their original LHD condition, which devalues them in the UK but has its attractions on the Continent, of course. Where a LHD car has been converted to RHD, even when the conversion has been carried out well, such cars do not attract quite the same value in the UK as an equivalent original RHD. Where the conversion to RHD has been inexpertly carried out the value will be further reduced.

A few cars were fitted with automatic gearboxes, and these are reduced in value by as much as 10-20% compared with equivalent specification manual cars.

A very tidy example of the Fixed-head.

Photographs of an original factory-made Sprint FHC are hard to come by, so I cheated – this is Gary Faqua's beautiful and nicely tuned DHC version.

The '4-speed' axle has a ring of bolts around the nose/pinion assembly, allowing it to be unbolted ...

... while the later, stronger, so called '5-speed,' axle does not.

A few TR7s remain with 4-speed gearboxes and the banjo rear axle and these are probably also reduced in value by 10-20% compared with equivalent specification 5-speed cars.

V8 models (note: new, 100% standard)
TR8 (genuine RHD) 100%
TR8 LHD Drop-head 90%
TR7-V8 conversion Drop-head 30-50%
TR7-V8 conversion Coupe 20-30%

Notes
Given there are so few genuine TR8s remaining in the UK, prices differ by quite large margins, with really good cars fetching ● x15,000. There is often little difference in price between UK and US versions.

When shopping watch for TR7-V8 conversions masquerading as genuine TR8s, and read the appendix and check the commission number if you are tempted.

The last estimate (2007) from the DVLA records 48 TR8s in the UK. However, some will be TR7-V8s that have managed to get TR8 on the log book, and may not be genuine.

Like original factory Sprints, factory-made RHD TR8s are few and far between, so this is what most UK 'TR8s' comprise: a TR7 V8 conversion – seen here nearing completion with Holley AFB carburetion. The forthcoming air filter fitment may be challenging. You will see the original carburetion arrangement shortly.

This is a genuine LHD TR8 Efi in concours condition owned by Jim TenCate in the US.

Wayne Walsh declares this to be a TR7 V8 conversion – but it's an exceptional one with a 5-litre Rover engine and Tremac T5 gearbox. Its value will be much higher than the average V8 conversion.

A not untypical FHC V8 conversion utilises an ex-Rover SD1 with original carburetion, as we see here.

13

5 Before you view
– be well informed

To avoid the frustration of a car not matching your expectations, remember to ask specific questions when you call before viewing. Excitement about buying a TR7 or TR8 can make even the most obvious things slip your mind, and it's harder for sellers to answer very specific questions dishonestly. Try to assess the attitude and demeanour of the seller, and decide how comfortable you are buying a used car from him or her.

Where is the car?
Work out the cost of travelling to view a car. For a rare model, or the exact specification you want, it may be worth travelling, but if your target is a common vehicle you should decide first how far you're prepared to go. Locally advertised cars can add to your knowledge for very little effort, so don't dismiss them.

Dealer or private sale?
Is the seller the owner or a trader? Private owners should have all the history and be happy to answer detailed questions. Dealers may know less about a car, but should have some documentation and may offer finance. If a dealer offers no warranty or guarantee in writing, then why not buy privately and save money?

Cost of collection and delivery?
Dealers may deliver but it probably won't be cheap. Private owners may meet you halfway, especially if the car is roadworthy, but be sure to view the car at the vendor's address beforehand to validate ownership and vehicle documentation.

Viewing, when and where?
It's always preferable to view at the vendor's home or business. A private seller's name and address should be on the title documents unless there's a good reason why not. Have at least one viewing in daylight and preferably dry weather. Most cars look better in poor light or when wet.

Reason for sale?
Genuine sellers will explain why they are selling and their length of ownership. They may also know something about previous owners.

RHD conversions
Many TR7 and TR8s have returned to Europe from the US. Conversion to RHD normally reduces their absolute value but makes them more saleable in the UK. Conversion can be easily verified since identification number suffixes, explored in Chapter 17, differed between RHD and LHD. Check if headlights, wiper pattern and sidelight colour are correct for your market, as some safety inspections insist on this. Ask about the carburettors and compression, because US market cars were given differing carburetion and emissions configurations from market to market, even within the overall North American market.

Condition (body/chassis/interior/mechanics)?
Query the car's condition in as specific terms as possible – preferably citing the checklist items described in Chapter 9.

All original specification?
An unmolested original car is invariably of higher value and sometimes easier to get spares for than a customised vehicle. If customised, ensure you get details of part numbers used.

Matching data/legal ownership
All TR7 and TR8s have a chassis number, body number, engine number, and gearbox number. All the numbers on the major parts and data plate should match to justify a top price, although changed engines, etc. noted on registration documents are acceptable, especially if the originals come with the car.

Does the vendor own the car outright or is money owed to a finance company or bank? Might the car even be stolen? Do any necessary finance checks before buying. Such companies can often also confirm if the car has ever been an insurance write-off. In the UK, the following organisations can supply vehicle data:

HPI   01722 422 422
AA   0870 600 0836
DVLA   0870 240 0010
RAC   0870 533 3660
Other countries will have similar organisations.

Roadworthiness
Does the car have all necessary certificates and/or comply with emissions rules? Test status for UK cars can be checked by phoning 0845 600 5977. Similar checks are available in some other markets.

If required, does the car carry a current road fund licence/license plate tag?

Unleaded fuel?
The four-cylinder TR7 and eight-cylinder TR8 engines (along with TR7 V8 Rover conversions) all have one important thing in common when it comes to the daily use of unleaded fuels – their cylinder head(s) are made from aluminium alloy and thus were originally fitted with hardened inserts to form the inlet and exhaust valve seats, making the heads suitable for the use of unleaded fuel. In fact, British Leyland, as with so many other details, actually led the world at that time, probably as a result of their heavy reliance on the US market generally and California, in particular.

TR7 exhaust valves, as well as those fitted to TR8 (and of course other Rover V8 engines of the day) were also able to withstand the unlubricated fuels (with lead) that were in general use in the mid-1970s. The use of unleaded fuels is okay, with two cautionary provisos: firstly, fuels develop very rapidly and today's unleaded will be very different to that of the 1970s, thus always use the best quality unleaded fuel available to you. Secondly, remember that, although TR7 and TR8 fuel lines were mostly made from sections of steel, short lengths of rubber hose were used to link the main fuel lines, filters and carburetors, so you would be prudent to check and upgrade these to modern unleaded compatible material (often plastic these days) if in any doubt as to their integrity.

Insurance

If intending to drive the car home, check with your existing insurer in case your current policy does not cover you. It's wise to check insurance costs before purchase in any case, as TR7s and TR8s are valuable and fast cars.

How you can pay

A cheque/check will take several days to clear and the seller may prefer to sell to a cash buyer. Cash can also be a valuable bargaining tool. However, a banker's draft or money order may be as good as cash, so ask beforehand. Paypal can provide the buyer some recourse if the vehicle is significantly mis-represented, as well as the option of using credit card for (expensive) financing.

Buying at auction?

Here is a list of auctioneers that could provide you with your dream car.
For information on buying at auction, see chapter 10.
Barrett-Jackson www.barrett-jackson.com
Bonhams www.bonhams.com
British Car Auctions www.bca-europe.com or www.british-car-auctions.co.uk
Cheffins www.cheffins.co.uk
Christies www.christies.com
Coys www.coys.co.uk
eBay www.ebay.com
H&H www.classic-auctions.co.uk
RM www.rmauctions.com
Shannons www.shannons.com.au
Silver www.silverauctions.com

Professional vehicle check

TR7s and TR8s are not complex cars by today's standards. Nevertheless, there are some important checks that should be made. If you feel unsure about making these checks yourself there are often marque/model specialists who will undertake professional examination of a vehicle on your behalf. Owner's clubs will be able to put you in touch with such specialists.

Other organisations that will carry out a general professional check in the UK are:

AA   0800 085 3007 (motoring organisation with vehicle inspectors)
ABS   0800 358 5855 (specialist vehicle inspection company)
RAC   0870 533 3660 (motoring organisation with vehicle inspectors)
Other countries will have similar organisations.

6 Inspection equipment

– these items will really help

This book

This book is designed to be your guide at every step, so take it along and use the check boxes in Chapter 9 to help assess each area. Don't be afraid to let the seller see you using it.

Glasses (if needed)

Take your reading glasses if you need them, to read documents and make close-up inspections. You will be prudent to take safety glasses and/or goggles if working under the car.

Magnet (not powerful, a fridge magnet is ideal)

A magnet will help you check if the car is full of filler, or has fibreglass panels, but be careful not to damage the paintwork. It's a rule of TR7s and TR8s that the rust you see is always far less than the hidden rust you cannot see. There's nothing wrong with a fibreglass bonnet/hood or boot/trunk lid, apart from the lowered value and, sometimes, paint finish. You will find the magnet particularly useful at the point where body panels meet. See Chapters 7 and 9 for a more comprehensive breakdown of the locations particularly vulnerable to corrosion, and where, consequently, body filler is popular.

Probe (a small screwdriver works very well)

A small screwdriver can be used – with care, and the owner's permission – as a probe, particularly on the inner and outer sills, rear lower quarters, boot/trunk floor, and anywhere around the bulkhead/firewall and battery tray to check any areas of corrosion.

Overalls

Be prepared to get dirty; take some overalls for getting under the car.

Mirror on a stick

Fixing a mirror at an angle on the end of a stick can help to check the condition of the underside of the car and some of the important areas around the chassis. You can also use it, together with a torch, at several points on the chassis and bodywork, detailed in Chapters 7 and 9. A full on-ramp inspection is ideal.

Torch

You could find a good torch/flashlight helps peering into dark recesses of the car even if you don't intend going underneath on this visit.

Digital camera

If possible, take a digital camera for reference or to study known trouble spots later. Show an expert pictures of any part that causes you concern. Ideally, have a friend or knowledgeable enthusiast accompany you: a second opinion is always valuable.

Sadly, it is an inescapable fact that all TRs have a number of corrosion weak spots. The welded seams (where two pressings overlap and are spot-welded) on TR7s and '8s were never given any factory rust protection nor, for that matter, were the inner faces of any of the panels or voids throughout the car. Consequently, water, salt, and mud splashes under and into the panels and seams to form a permanently damp 'skin' on or in the unprotected steel – making the wings/fenders, front turrets, sills/rockers, doors, indeed any TR7 body panel, vulnerable to corrosion along the seams and folded-over section.

The turrets are structurally very important, yet susceptible to corrosion – as you can guess from the extensive new panel-work and spot welding that has taken place here.

This is what a TR7 looks like with the front wing/fender removed, revealing an unprotected rust-prone void. This car is actually in better shape than most. Even so, the overlapped lip around the wheelarch is completely missing at the front, and the inner panel (top-right corner) is rusted through.

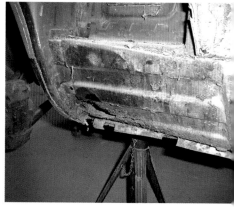

This picture shows the sill, or what remains of it. Your problem is that most of this corrosion is hidden from view and you have to picture what is likely behind the corrosion that you can see when you view the car.

The doors are rather easier to judge as the condition of the skin is in plain view (but did you spot the caked-on filler?) and you only need to open the door to see the condition of the frame. In this case the sill holds no secrets – shouting 'walk-away' to all but those seeking a set of spares or a restoration project.

As your inspection progresses remember that whatever corrosion you can actually see, since the corrosion inevitably occurs where two panels are welded together, there is probably at least as much corrosion hidden from view too! Some of the illustrations shown here are certainly on the dire side of what you may be offered, but they nevertheless serve to show you the sort of rust holes that can occur, and should alert you to watch for fillered cover-ups in the areas listed below. Most vulnerable spots are common to all models. Each should be examined carefully and a magnet used to test for body filler when in doubt.

Much of the inspection will require you to crawl underneath an elevated car. Dress accordingly, but above all ensure the car is *safely* jacked-up and securely positioned on axle stands. If in doubt, take your own axle stands, trolley jack, a powerful torch/flashlight and safety glasses.

Exterior

An overall impression of the car's bodywork is best obtained from the rear of the body; so kneel at each rear corner in turn to sight your eye down the sides of the car. The car should have a steady curve and there should be no significant ripples in any panel, which signal a knock and/or poor rebuild.

Check each of the opening panel gaps with the adjoining 'fixed' panel, in particular the door gaps with the adjoining 'B'-post, but right round the bonnet/hood, both doors, and the boot/trunk lid. These gaps should be even all the way round each opening panel. On a DHC if one or both rear door gaps close towards the top, the chances are that the sills/rockers are corroded and have lost much of their integrity. Be alert to the fact that corroded sills are often bodged with an over-sill, and that, even with generally otherwise well-maintained home cars, the inner strengtheners aren't replaced, as few people know they should be there. FHC viewers will need to look under the car for confirmation of a structural problem.

You will form an impression as to the extent to which rust has progressed throughout the bodywork if you check the following for rust, paint bubbling, body filler (use a magnet if unsure), or signs of local remedial attention:

• The four wing/fender panel joints where each panel interfaces with the scuttle at the front and the rear deck.
• Along the bottom of the doors (take great care to avoid sharp rusting metal edges).
• *Under* the front bumper generally, and under the front headlight apron panel.
• The exterior and interior of the sills/rockers. Internally where they adjoin the floor, lift the carpet and feel if it is damp/cold.
• Boot/trunk floor generally, the inner rear wheelarches, and the spare wheel-well in particular.

While you are doing these checks, take a few seconds to survey the overall quality of the paintwork and whether you like the colour. Consider: has this car recently been re-sprayed and if so, why?

Lastly, check the bumpers for damage or fading.

Under-bonnet/hood

Still interested? Lift the bonnet/hood and check the inner front wing/fenders and round the turrets for corrosion or recent attention. If OK, take a look down each gutter joint for corrosion (bad news) and for signs of pre-painted (and rust preventative wax coated) panels. Look particularly carefully at where the inner front

Ah! That's more like it ... wait a minute, or is it? Look at those patches behind the header tank, to the right of and at the bottom of the turret. The latter looks quite recent and suggests that the first batch of repairs didn't cover all the bases.

This suggests a proper/full/professional restoration. The void behind the front wing/fender has been repaired (with mostly new panels, judging by the view through the wheelarch), and then spray-painted. It will be hard to see this standard of care once the new front wing/fender is welded in place, but it's worth peering through any holes you can see through, or checking any restoration pictures the current owner offers.

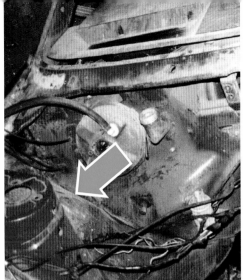

As a quick overall impression check, look here. Note the extensive corrosion around the inner-wing/fender and the bulkhead/firewall where water has been directed by the design of these panels and corrosion has set in. However, these turrets – another vulnerable part of the TR7/8 bodyshell – look to be in good shape.

The V8 engines in TR8s or TR7-V8 conversions are prone to oil-sludge and, thus, need oil/ filter changes every 3000 miles. Check here for cleanliness, confirming the engine has been well maintained.

wings meet the bulkhead/firewall. This is a notorious rust trap, exacerbated by the fact that it is not only hidden from view (by the brake servo/booster and battery tray) but the design of the pressings channels the water inward to this spot to form an ideal rust factory. Furthermore, it is complicated to repair.

Check the under-bonnet/hood paintwork matches the exterior paint colour and look closely for corrosion around the area where the battery is mounted. Now that the bonnet/hood is raised, check the four corners for corrosion inside and out.

Take a look round the engine bay for any signs of water or oil leaks. TR7 1998cc engines are prone to coolant leaks so dry, worse yet wet, anti-freeze around the cylinder head and/or water pump in particular, but anywhere in the engine-bay, is certainly possible and potentially an expensive repair. Whatever the engine, take a look at the oil level dipstick for clean-ish oil, but more particularly for white emulsified oil signalling coolant entering the oil system. Remove the water-pressure cap (assuming the engine is cold) and check for a very thin coloured layer of oil on top of the water. To check that the engine you are considering has been properly maintained, remove the oil-filler cap and check there is no white/thick sludge on the underside signalling minimum maintenance.

While you've got your head in the engine-bay and have torch in hand, make a note of the engine number.

If the TR7 1998cc engine prefix (details of commission number are in Chapter 17) does not match the supposed origin of the car, the 'originality' value can be adversely affected but maybe, in some cases, not severely. The engine has a weakness in that the head is usually difficult, sometimes impossible, to remove from the block without destroying it when cost and expediency necessitate a replacement engine. On occasions, similar looking engines are imported from Triumph Dolomite that considerably devalue the car unless it's a 16-valve Dolomite Sprint engine, which many would feel preferable to the original engine. Only you, the buyer, can decide whether you see that as an advantage or disadvantage.

How does the car go/sound/feel?

Assuming you're still interested and your insurance covers you, go for a short drive, during which you will be well advised to watch the temperature gauge for any signs of abnormality or overheating, and to find a hill to drive up if possible to stress the cooling system as far as you can in a short while. Do not worry about the car's tune or acceleration or finer details – we are initially looking for expensive problems. It must pull up straight on the brakes, not puff out smoke from the exhaust, change gear without balking or grating, steer straight ('hands-off' the steering wheel). Obviously, you also need to ensure there are no unpleasant noises or 'clonks' from the suspension (a common fault both at the front and rear), propshaft (this may sound as if it's coming from the gearbox or rear axle), the engine, gearbox or rear-axle areas of the car when accelerating, braking or turning.

Listen for a noisy timing chain or, worse, bearing rumble, and once back at base, if you have the slightest suspicion of timing chain noise or main bearing rumble, lift the bonnet again and use a long screwdriver as a stethoscope (take care to avoid all moving parts) to amplify and isolate the sound(s) and give you a clue as to whether engine refurbishment is 'on the cards.'

Try the gearbox briefly in each gear concentrating for now on testing the gear in over-run. The gear should stay engaged, but if it pops out the gearbox is worn. The 4-speed box should be pretty smooth but, ironically, the stronger more desirable 5-speed 'box normally feels 'notchy,' particularly when cold. Thus, once things are warm check 2nd gear for balking and synchromesh operation coming down the 'box, and whether there is any whine from the rear axle on drive or over-run.

Did the 'low-water level' warning light extinguish? Try as many electrical switches as practical in the time available but certainly the headlights. A shop window reflection is sometimes helpful to confirm things are working.

How did the brakes feel to you – did you feel they have 'bite' or did they fade after heavy applications?

Underneath

If this car still interests you, but with your safety at the forefront of your mind, look at the inside faces of the sills and chassis crossmembers by driving the rear of the car up onto a pair of ramps or by jacking the rear of the car up and securely placing axle stands under it. Take your torch and, if the current owner agrees, a small prodder (a screwdriver is ideal) and take a close check of the inside faces of the sills/rockers and the bottoms of the rear axle wheel recess, particularly where the floor meet the front heal-board. You must be sure that the main chassis members are free of serious corrosion and/or any patched repairs. The best test of the sills/rockers (only if the owner agrees) is to get the car back on the ground and, making absolutely sure you are clear of the car at all times, fit the car's jack in the jacking point below the centre of the sill. A solid sill and jacking point will allow you to raise each side of the car sufficiently to, say, change a wheel. A weakened sill will probably creak and groan its warning, while a corroded and unsatisfactory sill will almost certainly allow the jacking point to move upward into the sill and signal it is time to walk away from this one.

If you have the car up on ramps, take the opportunity to look at the front mounting points of all four rear suspension arms and the underside of the boot/trunk floor.

Take a look at the fuel tank and fuel lines. You may not see any significant external corrosion but look out (and sniff) for a fuel leak, taking great care because a hot light, such as a mains powered lead-lamp, can actually ignite any fuel droplets. Use a battery-powered torch/flashlight in this area.

Check that you do have a 5-speed rear axle in situ. It's best to avoid 4-speed axles.

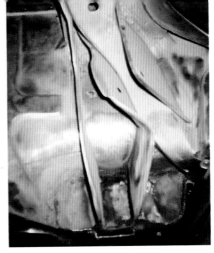

After considerable remedial work, this rear suspension to chassis mounting point (one of four) is in good order.

Interior

Take a quick look at the trim panels and carpets, although their condition should not materially influence your decision whether to meticulously explore the car as per Chapter 9. Collapsing seats may be a turn-off and a hassle to repair, but better a seat and trim refurbishment, in spite of new replacements not always being available, than an engine replacement, and much better than a bodyshell renovation and re-paint!

Paperwork

If you're still interested, this would be a good moment to check the registration document – the V5C in the UK and the Title in the US. First off, ensure that the person you are talking to and the address you are visiting crosscheck with the registration document. If they do not, you will need a very convincing explanation to retain your interest. You need then to check that the chassis number and engine numbers not only crosscheck with the registration document, but are also compatible with the year of the car and its model number. You will find this information in Chapter 17.

Is it worth staying for a longer look?

• Is the colour what you expected or can live with?
• Does the paintwork seem acceptable?
• Does the bodywork seem sound – bearing in mind a body and the consequential paint restoration is very expensive?
• Are you really able to rectify any shortcomings you've noticed or should you be taking advice as to what is involved before you decide?
• Although the easiest and least expensive to rectify, do the main mechanical components seem in reasonable order so far?
• Are the shortcomings you have discovered reflected in the price?
• Is your heart ruling your head? If so, come back after you've had time to think and maybe talk to a TR7 professional specialist. Best not to act in haste and regret at leisure!

8 Key points
– where to look for problems

This looks a good bet, although the TR7 bodywork demands that you never drop your guard ...

There is a welded patch in the top wing/ fender here, but more importantly, the seam between the wing and nose-cone shows no sign of good restoration practice. A full-on restoration would have this seam/ joint welded down its length, but in fact, the current arrangement does not look as if it's even had both inner faces of this seam pre-painted. The result will probably look good in the short-term but one wonders how it will stand the rigors of flexing and time.

... while, by now, you will realise that this is the sort of example that calls for great caution.

The trim can look very good indeed, even after 30-odd years, but is not the buy-or-not-buy factor.

These are the usual hidden corrosion weak spots on the Coupe – the 'B'-pillar and along the lower half of the screen seal.

Good brake upgrades, ideally behind enlarged wheels, are of significant benefit in the under-braked TR7-8 range.

The four-cylinder engines are slanted, offering lower under-bonnet/hood height but with coolant leakage and cylinder head removal difficulties.

The original TR8 and many subsequent V8 conversions fit the battery in the boot/trunk. Here is one rather better than average such fitting. Check that the feed cable to the starter motor is substantial.

This photo shows a TR7 V8 conversion utilising the later SD1/Range Rover intake plenum. Whilst such fuel-injection equipment offers wonderful performance and tuning potential, it can give the owner headaches when trying to fit the fresh air scoop (omitted here) and when the hot and fume-laden air from the engine compartment consequentially enters the cockpit.

The Sprint 16-valve cylinder head offers huge tuning potential by virtue of its 4-valves per cylinder breathing. The 8 (smaller) exhaust valves will go in on the right of this picture. The output of the original Sprint engine was inhibited by the design necessitating the use of one cam profile for both inlet and exhaust valves, which compromised the initial potential somewhat, although today's engine tuners do not seem overly restricted, producing prodigious power from Sprint engines.

9 Serious evaluation
– 60 minutes for years of enjoyment

Score each section as follows: 4 = excellent; 3 = good; 2 = average; 1 = poor
The totting up procedure is detailed at the end of the chapter. Be realistic in your
marking!

It's hard to remember the detail of any particular car you inspect on a serious basis,
even an hour or two later, never mind after you have explored 2 or 3 subsequent
cars, so use the tick boxes in each section as your evaluation progresses. Use
different colour pens for different cars, but be realistic and as consistent as possible
with your marking. Note that you may care to 'weight' the body and paintwork
marks for each car due to their particularly high rectification costs.

Instead of marking your pristine book you could photocopy these pages for each
car you plan to examine and write the VIN/registration/tag number at the top of
each page in order to retain a detailed reference for later comparisons. Alternatively,
Brad Wilson of Wedgeparts has a downloadable/printable check-sheet on his
website (www.wedgeparts.com) that mirrors this one.

Body panels
There is much to examine beneath the car, in fact the absence of paint, trim, and
body filler might make this the most telling area of your examination. You'll be
seeking signs of new panels and/or body corrosion certainly, but, as you progress
to the suspension mountings, fuel tank and the type of rear axle fitted, all this will
be much easier, quicker and more thorough if you can put the car on a local garage
ramp for a few minutes. Thus, if you are really serious about the car, it may be
worthwhile phoning the garage where the last annual test was carried out even if a
few minutes on their ramp costs a relatively small sum.

1.　　　　　　　　　　　　　　　　　　　　　4　3　2　1
Kneel down at each rear corner and sight your eye down the length of each side
of the car. The car should have a steady curve and there should be no significant
ripples in any panel that signal a knock and/or poor rebuild.

Paint, not necessarily in body colour, and wax
injection should both be well in evidence in as
many of the car's voids as you can see. With the
headlight pods in place, the void behind this front
cone will be less easy to access, and trim will
restrict your access to the doors. You might see
something inside the wing voids using a mirror
and torch/flashlight.

2.　　　　　　　　　　　　　　　　　　　　　4　3　2　1
Explore bodyshell voids for the corrosion protection that any properly restored/
maintained shell should now enjoy.

If the outside of this rear deck to rear wing/fender looks bad, wait until you look at it from inside the boot/trunk. What you are looking for on a restored car is only a very shallow and certainly a rust-free seam on top of each wing/fender, while on un-restored examples search as far into the seam as possible for rust or a superficial local repair.

3. ☒ ☒ ☒ ☒

A second check on the thoroughness, or otherwise, of a restored shell is that the seams between each of the four wings/fenders and their respective mating panels have been seam-welded, and a mock seam chased into the joint, which ensures longevity of the restoration.

At the front of the car the problems are exactly the same, although here some local preparation is taking place – but the faces of the wing and its mating panel will remain unprotected.

Road spray and debris is forced into the wheelarch and turret, which form very effective corrosion traps, exacerbated by the internal brackets bolted inside the turret. There should be no signs of corrosion like this, welding, or patched repairs.

4. ☒ ☒ ☒ ☒

The full length of the seams between each of the front wings/fenders and the shell are a good place to get a general impression as to the quality of the restoration or the extent of corrosion in the car you are viewing. Look right down the full length of the mating joint from the scuttle to the front of the nose cone.

5. ☒ ☒ ☒ ☒

The condition of both front suspension mounting turrets and the adjacent/mating panels is crucial, and will need close examination. Not only do these parts of the shell form part of the front suspension geometry, they contribute to the structural strength of the front of the car, too.

6. ☒ ☒ ☒ ☒

With the owner's agreement, take a small sharp probe and check for rot around the rear trailing arm mountings – where they meet the floorpan and feed stresses into the rear bulkhead.

Corrosion around the rear suspension mountings is obviously totally unsatisfactory. Here, a start has been made at cutting away the corrosion before new panels are fitted.

7.

Reach up and feel (with care) the top of both chassis leg box-sections adjacent to the tops of the rear dampers for corrosion.

There is absolutely no problem here, but check the tops of both rear dampers because the car you're viewing may not be this good.

8.

While there, although not a bodyshell issue, double check that a 5-speed axle *is* fitted.

The 5-speed rear axle has the front of the pinion casing cast integrally with the main axle housing.

9.

From under the rear of the car, check the rear of each floorpanel and the rear bulkhead/kick-panel. This area is vulnerable to corrosion generally, but particularly around the structural strengthening section behind the bulkhead that forms a two-panel corrosion trap and rots out the bulkhead and adjacent panels.

This shot is actually of an area a few inches further forward of where your check should be but, nevertheless, shows a floor patch (top edge of picture), some jacking damage, and a solid looking rear suspension mounting in the bottom left corner. The sills/rockers look good, too, so by and large a 'pass' – although I'm not sure about that fuel line route and fastening.

10.

While under the car, give the brake pipes across the rear axle the once-over. The original 'bundy' pipes will long since have been replaced, but the replacements (unless they are 'copper') may have corroded. Any pitting will necessitate replacements. You'll get a view of the vulnerable axle-mounted pipes in the picture to point 6 under the heading 'Road testing.'

11.

The inner and outer sill pressings provide crucial structural integrity to the car and both sides need to be examined closely. You'll get a general impression by close inspection of the inside and outside, initially at the rear, but you can also push down on each back wing of the DHC while looking at the door gaps. There will inevitably be some movement, even in a perfectly sound car, perhaps one millimetre, but if you can see more than this minimal movement the inner sills will have lost their structural integrity.

In contrast to the previous picture, these sills/rockers are clearly going to require replacement.

12.

At the front, the sills are exposed and vulnerable to corrosion from the outside, but, additionally, water runs down the gutter below the windscreen/ windshield into the originally unpainted void behind the front wing/fender.

Consequently, look for sill corrosion under the front of the car, along the bottom of the front wing/fenders, and inside the car, because the rot can spread through the front of the inner sill to the outside edges of the floors. Obviously, the rot will also spread backwards along the bottom of the sills/floor once the water has access to the sill void.

13.

While there, although not a bodyshell issue, examine both front brakes. TR7 (including Sprint) discs were 241mm diameter (9½in) by 9.5mm width. The discs on TR8s were 244mm diameter by 14.3mm width and should be fitted as a minimum, not only on the TR8 but to V8 conversions, too (and, in my opinion, Sprints and conversions). You will not be able to measure the diameter but all discs should be full-width to the edge, un-scored, and of normal/shiny colour. If they are thin, scored, crazing, and blue (the latter the result of overheating) you have not only an urgent brake repair on your hands but an upgrade too – if you are prudent.

14.

The front windscreen/windshield has two vulnerable areas, both of which are unfortunately largely hidden from view during your pre-purchase inspection. The first area allows water to leak past the windscreen/windshield, corroding the inner lip of the 'screen frame.

Not all windscreen seal corrosion will be so evident, but it's worth looking round the edge of the seal for any evidence.

Similarly, this restoration candidate shows a fairly extreme case of scuttle corrosion below the 'screen, but proves it is worth looking closely in this vulnerable area, too.

15.

Rainwater can also corrode the scuttle panel through which the wiper spindles pass, but this, too, is hidden from view by a piece of black trim. Look for signs of corrosion, mostly outboard of the wiper spindles, and check the carpets for water damage or dampness signalling that the inside-out rust has holed the scuttle panel and is letting water into the footwells. A holed scuttle panel means you should walk-away from this car (checking the footwell carpets for wet/dampness has a dual purpose in that the rear of the front inner wings [where they join the bulkhead] is a very common rust trap, too, causing the internal matting at the front to become wet for no apparent reason).

16.

The inner wing channel down each side of the engine bay needs checking for corrosion.

The gutter and top seam between the inner and outer wing/fender are attacked from both sides and are susceptible to corrosion.

17.

While your head is in the engine bay, check the two main chassis rails just in front of the front suspension subframe. It the car has been in a hefty frontal shunt there is likely to be some wrinkling or distortion of either or both rails.

This is a superb 'absolutely no problem' example but, although probably greasy and possibly wet, nevertheless it's worth just running your hand along each rail for about 12in (300mm) in front of the front subframe mounting bolts as you may feel ripples that are not easily visible. Also, from under the car, check for rust in the rails around the mounting points of the subframe.

18.

Feel (very carefully) inside both front wheelarches, particularly if there is bubbling in evidence. Corrosion in the outer lips of the wheelarches is easy to temporarily hide with body filler, but the inner panel lip rarely gets remedial attention and is where you will get a truer picture of the situation. Be particularly alert if the rust bubbles extend up the outer wing.

19.

Examine the lips to the rear wings/fenders equally closely by the same (careful) method.

This is a rear wheelarch but, front or back, this is what you do not want to see, nor do you want to suspect that this has been superficially bodged over before you got to see the car. You'll probably get a clue by feeling (very carefully) the inner arch where it's unlikely to have been touched. Examples like this almost certainly require a new inner and outer wing/fender because mud and water will have penetrated the void between the inner and outer panels and created a major rust trap. Sadly, the situation is *always* worse than it appears!

20.

The nose cone assembly can corrode in several places, and you should check for body filler since they are expensive to replace. The panel just in front of the bonnet/hood needs to be examined, as does the lower front valance/spoiler.

Although this example looks good, the front panels are particularly vulnerable to rust at both ends where they join the flitch panels, at the middle-strengthening panel (just out of shot), and as the result of minor accident damage. I like it, but think this is a fibreglass aftermarket valance, which some viewers may not be comfortable about. Original cars had a pressed metal valance with a plastic spoiler across the bottom.

21.

The front bulkhead/firewall requires examination in four places: on both left and right sides of the car; both sides of the panel; where the inner wings join the bulkhead is particularly vulnerable; while the battery tray acts a further corrosion trap, as we saw in Chapter 7's illustrations (see page 21).

22.

With the bonnet open so that you can check it inside and out, look for paint blistering and/or body filler repairs to any or all four corners. These will quickly crack from the bonnet slamming and flexing.

I doubt you'll see anything as bad as this, but any paint blistering you see from the outside in any/all four corners of the bonnet/hood tells you that the corrosion is well advanced. Post 1979 (double-hump) bonnets rust particularly badly. Note the corrosion inside the headlight void, and, of course, down this wing/cone seam.

An exemplary headlight pod after restoration.

23.

The headlight pods are alloy and susceptible to paint bubbling or flaking. They will need sandblasting, etch-priming and re-painting if you find corrosion.

24.

Take a look, inside and out, at the lower-rear edge of the boot-lid where the panel has been folded over on itself. Water gets into the seam and opens it up, allowing more water in and accelerating the corrosion trap.

25.

While in that area, lift a small section of the rubber lip seal around the boot opening to see if corrosion has established itself in the seams. Corrosion would be so advanced that you hardly need to lift the rubber seal – but that was where this problem started.

26.

This floor drain hole was probably used primarily during the bodyshell's manufacture, and is normally closed off with a circular plate. The drain holes you need to ensure are open are considerably smaller in diameter than seen here.

No problem with these drain holes being blocked.

27.

We covered looking at the outside of the rear wing/fender's top seam very early in your check list, but it now needs inspection from inside the boot/trunk. While examining the rear top deck from the underside, check the fuel filler as the plastic cover prevents you seeing from the outside the consequences of there being no drain holes in this recessed part of the panel.

The metalwork looks absolutely fine inside this boot/trunk but do, nevertheless, check that there are no unacceptable sharp metal seams across the front of the boot/trunk (behind the sagging trim). Unusually, the floor covering and fibreboard side trims are in place and look in excellent shape.

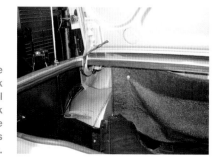

I could not find a shot of the inside of the spare wheel-well but this shows it admirably from the outside. A number of otherwise very solid cars have minor spare wheel-well corrosion, so in isolation it is not a cause for concern.

28. [4] [3] [2] [1]
The boot/trunk floor needs thorough examination. It has a chassis rail running each side beneath the floor, which form water traps and corrodes the floorpanel from below. The spare wheel-well creates a further double-skin corrosion trap, and the two side wells suffer both from internal condensation and the leaking boot seals mentioned earlier.

29. [4] [3] [2] [1]
The rear light panel, where it is welded to the boot, forms the now familiar double-skinned rust trap along the whole width of the car. Originally there would have been (card) trim panels protecting the rear lights from the contents of the boot – are they in place?

30. [4] [3] [2] [1]
The doors have three drain holes in the bottom of each frame. These can get

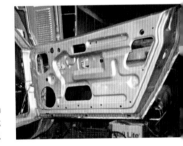

blocked with debris and cause water to build up within the door. Thus, there may be some, hopefully superficial, corrosion along the bottoms of each frame and on either/both door skins, and you need to ask yourself whether, after cleaning-up, they are corroded to the point of needing patch-repairs and/or re-skinning.

The three drain holes in the bottom of the doors are in plain view. If you own a TR7 it's a good idea to check these are clear, say, once a year.

31. [4] [3] [2] [1]
Check that both doors open smoothly, without stiffness that could signal seized/frozen hinges. Check, too, that they will shut smoothly without the need to lift the handle/door. The latter signals that at least one hinge, probably the lower, is worn, and rectification will likely involve welding a replacement in place – although if you're studying a Roadster's doors you may find that they are initially hard to open, a problem usually brought about by rusted/seized security fittings on the 'B'-post(s), or that the sills/rockers are badly corroded.

32. (FHC only) [4] [3] [2] [1]
Check the rear window surround/seal for signs of water ingress, and the internal trim below the window for dampness.

33. (FHC only) [4] [3] [2] [1]
The factory-fitted fabric sunroof on FHCs is prone to leaks, resulting in the roof

rotting at the rear corners when the drain holes become blocked. Check the operation of the sunroof and the corners of the aperture. There were also a variety of after-market sunroofs fitted that naturally need your close attention, too. Note, also, that sunroof apertures have been sheeted over and/or filled with varying degrees of professionalism, but all probably to hide a corroded roof structure.

Paintwork and trim

1. ⁴ ³ ² ¹
The external colour of the car – is it to your liking?

If you've got it, flaunt it, or so the saying goes – so I love the informative registration/tag plate!

This is the sort of paint finish to aim for.

2. ⁴ ³ ² ¹
The appearance of the paintwork is important and can vary enormously. How do you rate this car's appearance, bearing in mind the high cost of a re-spray?

3. ⁴ ³ ² ¹
Applied correctly, as a thin skim over a steel repair patch welded to solid original metal, plastic body filler is a wonderful aid and indispensable in the preparation of a local body repair prior to painting. However, it is sometimes miss-used when the solid steel panel patch of a local repair is bodged or omitted and the filler stuffed into a gaping hole or over the top of a latticework of rusting metal. Sooner or later, this short-cut and extremely bad practice will re-emerge;

This is how body filler should be used in preparation for a perfect paint job. Obviously, the vulnerable areas listed under the 'Body panel' heading are high-alert spots, but need not be the only areas where excessive body filler has been applied as a short-term fix. Be particularly suspicious about a car that has recently been re-sprayed, possibly, but not necessarily, to cover a multitude of sins. If in any doubt, use a magnet to ascertain whether the depth of filler at that point is excessive. If so, try other vulnerable places.

initially as cracking round the periphery of the 'repair' and in due course as a piece of filler falling out of an enlarged hole. This is a buyer-beware situation because, for a short period of time after the re-sprayed 'repair'/restoration, the panel(s) can look fairly presentable so you need to be on your guard for slight imperfections, ripples or other clues as to whether excessive body filler is present.

4. ☑4 ☑3 ☑2 ☑1

Do you like the colour of the internal trim (ie seats, panels, and carpets)?

My taste is for plainer colours but if you seek originality, or to replace a badly worn piece of trim, there are lots of used alternatives out there.

5. ☑4 ☑3 ☑2 ☑1

How do the seats feel (particularly the driver's seat)? Nice and firm or collapsing thus offering little support from the base cushion and/or the backrest?

The rubber seat base diaphragm seen here regularly gives way after years of use and, provided the base cover or cushion are in good shape, can be replaced, rejuvenating the base of the seat. The rear/backrests are not quite so straightforward because the rear seat cover has first to be removed to allow replacement of the rubber cross-strips, whereupon the seat cover is replaced. However, unsupportive seats should not put you off buying an otherwise sound car.

6. ☑4 ☑3 ☑2 ☑1

What do you think of the quality/wear etc of the internal trim? Some tartans (red and the green base colours) along with the two-tone black/ grey trims are very difficult to purchase new so, if their condition is poor and originality matters to you, mark this detail down severely and start looking for used parts.

Beautiful; no-one could complain about that quality. Check that the courtesy light works, though – it can be 'difficult'.

7. (DHCs only) ☑4 ☑3 ☑2 ☑1

How does the colour, quality and standard (ie wear and tear) of the hood sit with you?

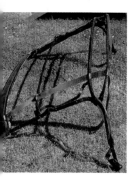

The hood frame is prone to seizing at numerous joints, whereupon an unfeeling owner forces the hood forward or back and bends/twists the frame, after which it never quite comes over smoothly or square.

8. (DHCs only) [4] [3] [2] [1]
Does the hood mechanism function smoothly?

Note: Do not buy or reject a car on the basis of its hood, seats, carpets, and internal lining panels. A poor car beautifully trimmed is not a good buy, while conversely, a sound car with tatty trim is worth purchasing at the right price. New hoods, seat recovering, carpets, indeed complete trim kits, are readily available so, even if you hate the colour or quality of the trim, this should not over-influence your decision to purchase an otherwise high quality car, although you will naturally use the trim as a bargaining opportunity.

Electrical tests

1. [4] [3] [2] [1]
Test the headlights when examining a TR7 or '8. Not to put too fine a point on the issue, but the headlights tend to be (fairly frequently) unreliable, with one or the other failing to come up, usually due to corroded wiring connectors and faults within the electric lifting motors. Switch the headlights on and off several times to check they operate every time and simultaneously. Check that they rise and fall in parallel with each other, that the headlight flasher works, and that the pods do not bind or are noisy in operation.

The headlight/pod lift motor, seen from under the car as you may view it. The mechanism and loom electrical connections are exposed to the weather and either/both can become corroded.

2. [4] [3] [2] [1]
The car's several earth/ground connections to the bodyshell are vulnerable to corrosion. Check by testing the side and taillights work satisfactorily, and at full brightness when several related lights are used (ie the brake lights and a flashing directional signal) in the same cluster.

3. [4] [3] [2] [1]
Check that all the interior lights, including the vulnerable in-door interior lights and boot lights, are operational.

4. [4] [3] [2] [1]
Check the dashboard and steering column switches as best you can by switching each one on and off several times, ensuring that each feels as if it has operated satisfactorily and that the electrical component in question is reacting appropriately.

A superb example of the dashboard/fascia, instruments, and steering wheel. Although this car is unlikely to present any problems, you still need to check the operation of the, sadly, unreliable switches and instruments, particularly the temperature gauge seen bottom-left of the instrument cluster.

Mechanical matters

Non-US cars had a compression ratio of 9.25:1. Cars destined for non-US markets were fitted with twin SU HS6 carburettors and generated 105bhp. Most US cars had a pair of Zenith-Stromberg carburettors, which were not as inefficient as is thought by some. However, these engines had lower compression ratios and the emission control equipment also required increased fuel consumption and reduced the power to no better than 92bhp. Early Californian cars had a single Stromberg carburettor, although post-1980 cars destined for California enjoyed Bosch L-Jetronic fuel-injection (which was also fitted to Japanese, Australian, and Canadian exports) and was extended to most US states from 1981.

This is a very nice example of the twin-SU engine sitting in a clean, solid, rust-free car.

The Sprint's 16-valve cylinder head design was both brilliant and restricted in that the same cam lobe operated the exhaust-valve (top of this picture) and, via a rocker arm, the inlet-valve. Thus, the cam profile was somewhat of a compromise. Subsequent engine tuners have, however, increased the engine's output making a good Sprint conversion a very attractive proposition.

The four-cylinder TR7 and Sprint engines

The TR7 used a four-cylinder engine of 1998cc with, for its day, an advanced design, incorporating an overhead cam and an alloy cylinder head unit that was inclined at 45° toward the left side of the car. A variant was jointly developed and used by Saab in its 99 model. Triumph also used the basic engine design in its Dolomite range, where it had smaller bores and 1850cc.

The Sprint engine was very similar (and requires basically the same evaluation as mentioned above) but was fitted with a very clever 16-valve cylinder head. Thus, whichever four-cylinder engine you are examining, your checks should start with a cold engine and progress as follows:

1.   [1]

Open the bonnet/hood and check for any signs of water, anti-freeze staining or oil leaks. TR7 1998cc engines are prone to coolant leaks, overheating, and head

warping, so dry, worse yet wet, coolant around the cylinder head and/or water pump in particular, but anywhere in the engine-bay, needs marking down severely.

Coolant leaks, overheating, and head-warping are this engine's nemesis and the arrowed face between head and block deserves your particularly close inspection.

2.   4 3 2 1
The first of a trio of cylinder head checks necessitates you look at the oil-level dipstick; both for oil level and colour. Dark, heavily carbon-laden oil signals poor maintenance, but more importantly you're checking that the oil is not white/ emulsified/milky, which signals coolant is getting into the oil system – probably as a consequence of a head gasket or warped cylinder head. Bearing in mind the potential cost/difficulty of the TR7 cylinder head problems, double check this detail by removing the oil-filler cap and looking under it for signs of emulsification.

3.   4 3 2 1
Remove the water-pressure cap (assuming the engine is cold) atop the expansion tank and check the water level and for a very thin, coloured layer of oil on top of the water, which signals oil is entering the coolant (more head problems in all likelihood). Check, too, that the anti-freeze content appears adequate.

The best of several designs of pressurised coolant header tank. If the engine appears to be running with very dilute anti-freeze the internal coolant passages may have corroded, for want of the anti-freeze's corrosion inhibitors, and/or the engine has a leak that required frequent top-ups and the owner has used pure water.

4.   4 3 2 1
The original cooling fan's viscous coupling is difficult to check comprehensively but should have *no* play back and forth. With the engine cold and stopped, try to spin the fan. It must not be seized solid, nor must it have absolutely no resistance to your spinning the blades. You're seeking a rather subjective halfway feel about it!

5.   4 3 2 1
The final cylinder head check necessitates the vendor starting the engine while you observe the colour of the exhaust. White exhaust smoke/steam will usually be noted if there is a cylinder head problem, dark oily exhaust probably signals general wear in the engine (you could put the palm of your hand a couple of inches from the pipe for confirmation), while black spotted smoke suggests worn or badly adjusted carburettors. Possibly this is the time to walk away, or at least re-negotiate the price if everything else is found to be in order.

6.

Now that the engine is running, listen for any rattling, usually from one or both of two locations; the cam buckets/tappets down the length of the cylinder head and the timing chain at the front of the engine.

This cut-away at S+S Preparations shows how near to the top of this engine the camshaft runs, as well as the valve operation via a bucket. New/oversized buckets of the correct size may not be available and, in any event, fitting them is a time consuming professional repair and, thus, expensive. The timing chain, its top sprocket, and some of its guides are very clearly seen and these are best replaced every 25k miles. While this is probably a home repair for the more practical, nevertheless, ask the vendor when the chain was last replaced and adjust the price of the car according to his answer and copy invoice.

7.

Once warmed up, the main bearings can rumble in worn engines and there is no easy way to check the oil pressure, so listen carefully for a bottom-end deep rumble, particularly if the car appears to have had minimal servicing or demonstrated an oily exhaust.

The V8 engine

If you're looking at a genuine TR8 (lucky you, for they are few and far between), or a TR7 converted to accept a V8 engine, the beautiful V8 engine should run smoothly and allow you to pull-away in top gear with little more than 1000rpm on the tachometer. It is a hardy and lightly-loaded engine quite capable of 150,000 miles between major re-builds – provided it has been properly serviced along the way. They do have two faults; they can wear out camshafts (and therefore the hydraulic cam followers) in 50,000 miles, even when regularly serviced, and also generate an above average amount of black engine sludge, necessitating oil changes at 3000 mile intervals. Consequently, the first two checks below are particularly relevant:

1.

Remove the oil filler cap from the front corner of the rocker-cover and, with a torch, take a look inside the rocker cover and at the inside of the oil filler cap (seen on page 21) for a build up of dark brown or black deposits signalling poor maintenance.

An original and immaculate TR8 fitted with some emissions equipment and air-conditioning, and inducted via a pair of pent-angled Stromberg carburettors. I doubt you'd find any such problems here, but other examples may show white emulsified oil/water deposits if a head gasket has blown (not unknown, particularly if the head has not been torqued to the latest recommendations) under the orange oil-filler cap.

2.

Check for oil in the water (another sign of a blown head gasket).

3.

Check that the front of the V8 engine is properly installed via brackets welded to the front subframe, and walk away from anything where the front engine mountings are welded to the chassis side rails.

4.

Even with a satisfactory front engine mounting, if the car is a V8 conversion, ask if there is an engineer's report on the car and study it closely. Ensure any criticisms have been corrected.

There are some excellent purpose-built V8 conversion kits (sold by Robsport International, S+S Preparations and/or Rimmer Bros), and you would be prudent to ensure that the conversion was carried out using one of these professional kits, and to examine the relevant receipts. At the heart of each kit will be the modified V8 engine mounting (seen here painted blue), specially fabricated to fix the engine to the subframe at the correct height. This engine is an ex-SD1 unit.

It's a joke! The smoke is coming from this powerful V8 conversion's burn-out, not the exhaust but ...

5.

The final cylinder head check necessitates the vendor starting the engine while you observe the colour of the exhaust. White exhaust smoke/steam will usually be noted

if there is a cylinder head problem, dark oily exhaust probably signals general wear in the engine (you could put the palm of your hand a couple of inches from the pipe for confirmation), while black spotty smoke suggests worn or badly adjusted carburettors.

6.

Listen for a 'missing' cylinder, possibly signalling the reduced, occasionally flat, cam lobe we touched upon earlier or ignition problems. You can sometimes feel the miss with you hand close to each exhaust pipe. Rev the engine a little – it'll be sluggish with a cylinder (or two) missing – they will likely still 'miss.' Best to presume and mark for the worst case but bear in mind that the swarf from the missing cam lobe has been circulating within the engine lubricant accelerating general wear (which makes your earlier maintenance frequency checks doubly relevant).

7.

Check there are no signs of interference between the top of the carburettors and the underside of the bonnet/hood, and that the bonnet closes completely and without the need for undue care.

... this is no joke because this SD1 engine is sitting too high in the engine bay and, obviously, the bonnet/hood will not close until the engine is lowered by, I guess, several inches (perhaps 50 to 75mm). This is often partly achieved by fitting short spacers between the front subframe and the chassis, but there are other changes necessary here.

Road testing

If you've checked the car out at the local garage, take at least 30 minutes on the return journey (or go for at least a 30-minute drive) because this is an opportunity to assess the general driving characteristics of the car, particularly:

1.

Watch the temperature gauge closely on any of the models under discussion and check that the 'low water' warning light extinguishes itself.

A climbing gauge indicates engine-cooling problems – common in TR7s and not unknown with V8 conversions.

Ask questions if the rev-counter/tachometer shows much above 2800rpm when the car is in 5th gear travelling at an indicated 70mph. A V8 car without a 3.08 ratio rear-axle will accelerate *very* quickly but rev excessively at motorway speeds and, consequently, will be expensive to run due to its high fuel consumption. Here the re-calibrated speedometer and the clock are being replaced, the latter by, to my mind, a preferable oil pressure gauge.

2.

Check that the other instruments work smoothly and, if you are driving a V8 conversion, that the tacho reflects that rear axle ratio has been upgraded.

3.

Try the brakes, initially gently from slow speed, but thereafter a number of times with progressively increasing road speed and ferocity provided no uncomfortable noises or characteristics come to light. Does the car pull-up in a straight line every time, does the front of the car dive under braking, and do the brakes 'bite' well enough to stop the car within a reasonable distance. Do they 'fade' after repeated fierce applications?

4.

Check the operation of the handbrake, either on a hill or against the drive of the engine; it is prone to seizure/freezing.

5.
Check for the car's reaction to hard acceleration. Does it bring about a steady drift to one side, that, on lifting off, is reversed as the car pitches to the other side, suggesting worn rear suspension trailing arm bushes.

You cannot actually see the front trailing-arm bush as it's hidden by metalwork, but the acceleration test will reveal any weaknesses and whether it will be necessary to change all eight bushes (four front attached to the bodyshell, and four at the back attached to the axle).

6.

Check both road springs and suspension bushes by finding a twisting back/country road and note any tendency for indirect steering, body-roll, and any feeling of instability while driving safely but enthusiastically.

This shot illustrates several areas of the rear suspension that you need to be thinking about as you road test this car.

7.

Can you hear a knocking noise from the rear of the car, probably signifying that the

mounting bolt hole(s) for one or more of the trailing arm(s) has worn oval? In this event, you will need to budget for welding washers to the bodyshell before re-fitting the trailing arms (with new bushes, of course) and/or tie-bars.

This is a 5-speed axle; included here to illustrate three of the four suspension to axle mounting points and slightly bigger brake drums.

8.

Listen for a noisy (mushy) manual gearbox which, if excessive, could signal low oil level, worn bearings, or slippage in autoboxes. Assume and mark for the worst case.

9.

Try the gearbox in every gear on over-run (not in drive) for jumping out of gear.

10.

The four-speed box should be reasonably smooth by 1980's standards, allowing swift/easy gear changes. Five-speed gearboxes tend to be a bit notchy in all gears, particularly going into second gear, but after you've tried a couple you will get the feel of this much stronger gearbox, and can mark it appropriately. If either gearbox is difficult to get into several gears (including second), the 'box may have the wrong lubricating oil, but, more likely, the clutch will be worn or the 'box needs an overhaul. Certainly, if either 'box refuses to go into a gear or makes complaining noises as it does, you have a serious/expensive clutch or gearbox problem, and you should mark accordingly.

11.

You can check the clutch release bearing part of the clutch assembly by, with the engine running and the gearbox in neutral, depressing the clutch. If the gearbox hisses, the clutch release bearing must be suspect and may necessitate a new clutch.

12. □ □ □ □

The 5-speed boxes have one weak point, revealed by a very pronounced growling noise when the engine is running with the 'box in neutral and the clutch pedal not depressed. The noise will disappear when you depress the clutch, and this will mean that the front (input) shaft roller-bearing is worn. If the gearbox has been in use for some time in this worn state, the gears within the 'box will also have become worn and the box may not be economically repaired. You can hardly drain the oil while inspecting the car, but, should you subsequently drain such a 'box, the swarf in the oil will tell its own story.

13. □ □ □ □

Check for rear-axle whine in acceleration, over-run, and in light driving conditions. The 5-speed axle is rather more prone to whine than the 4-speed axle, although any whine should not be interpreted as signalling imminent failure, but it is tiring on long journeys and sooner or later is best addressed.

The 4-speed axle that is less prone to whine. It is shown here upside down.

14. □ □ □ □

Check the wheels, particularly if they are alloys, for kerbing or corrosion, and, naturally, the tyres for wear and any wall bulging.

The original alloy wheels are really very attractive when restored, but be particularly wary of any uneven tyre wear across the width of the tread because that could be the result of poor tracking (a very easy adjustment) or an accident-damaged front end. Assume the worst. We saw an example of the steel wheel earlier on page 31.

Evaluation procedure

Add up the total points; they should be the same for any variant regardless of engine, FHC or DHC.
Score: 256 = excellent; 192 = good; 128 = average; 64 = poor.

Cars scoring over 179 will be completely useable and will require only maintenance and care to preserve condition. Cars scoring between 64 and 130 will require serious restoration (at much the same cost regardless of score). Cars scoring between 131 and 178 will require very careful assessment of necessary repair/restoration costs in order to arrive at a realistic value.

10 Auctions
– sold! Another way to buy your dream

Auction pros & cons
Pros: Auctions are where dealers buy and sell, so they operate as trade rather than retail markets. This means that, except for the so-called 'Prestige' auctions, prices are often lower than those on dealer premises and from some private sellers, so you could grab a bargain on the day. Auctioneers have usually confirmed ownership title with the seller, and at the venue it should be possible to check this and any other relevant paperwork. You may also receive 24 hours of warranty cover.
Cons: You can normally only get either minimal information before travelling to the venue, or vague and sometimes very sales-orientated descriptions. To avoid disappointment, learn to read between the lines of the catalogue or website description, and only visit if there are several candidate cars. Star lots may be stored indoors under good light, but even so, there is limited scope to examine the cars thoroughly.

Which auction?
Auctions by established auctioneers are advertised in the car magazines and on the auction houses' websites. A catalogue, or a simple printed list of the lots for auction might be available only a day or two ahead, though often lots are listed and pictured on auctioneers' websites much earlier. Contact the auction company to ask if previous auction selling prices are available as this is useful information (details of past sales are often available on websites).

Catalogue, entry fee & payment details
When you purchase the catalogue of the cars in the auction, it often acts as a ticket allowing two people to attend the viewing days and the auction, so take a friend; it's amazing what a second pair of eyes can spot. Catalogue details tend to be comparatively brief, but will include information such as 'one owner from new, low mileage, full service history,' etc. It will also usually show a guide price to give you some idea of what to expect to pay, and will tell you what is charged as a buyer's premium. The catalogue will also contain details of acceptable forms of payment. At the fall of the hammer an immediate deposit is usually required, the balance payable within 24 hours. If you plan to pay by cash, note that there may be a cash limit. Some auctions will accept payment by debit card. Sometimes credit or charge cards are acceptable, but will often incur an extra charge. A bank draft or bank transfer will have to be arranged in advance with your own bank, as well as with the auction house. No car will be released before all payments are cleared. If delays occur in payment transfers then storage costs can accrue.

Buyer's premium
A buyer's premium will be added to the hammer price – don't forget this in your calculations, or the extra 5-10% may come as a shock. It's not unusual for there to be a further state tax or local tax on the purchase price and/or on the buyer's premium.

Viewing

In some instances it's possible to view on the day, or days before, as well as in the hours prior to the auction. The wise buyer gets to the venue early and would do well to take this book, a mirror, and a torch. For nearby venues, try to arrive early on any preview days to see the lots arriving and being off-loaded or marshalled into position.

There are auction officials available who are willing to help out if need be. While the officials may unlock doors, engine and luggage compartments for inspection, or start the engine for you, a test ride is out of the question. Crawling under and around the car as much as you want is permitted, but you may not jack up a vehicle – hence the need for a mirror on a stick. Intended as trade sales, the cars often need valeting, which dealers are happy to do and should not put you off. You can also ask to see any available documentation.

Bidding

Before you take part in the auction, decide your maximum bid ... and stick to it! It may take a while for the auctioneer to reach the lot you're interested in, so use that time to observe how other bidders behave. When it's the turn of your car, attract the auctioneer's attention and make an early bid. The auctioneer will then look to you for a reaction every time another bid is made. Usually the bids will be in fixed increments until the bidding slows, when smaller increments will often be accepted before the hammer falls. If you want to withdraw from the bidding, make sure the auctioneer understands your intentions – a vigorous shake of the head when he or she looks to you for the next bid should do the trick!

Assuming that you're the successful bidder, the auctioneer will note your card or paddle number, and from that moment on you will be responsible for the car.

If it's unsold, either because it failed to reach the reserve or because there was little interest, it may be possible to negotiate with the owner, via the auctioneers, after the sale is over.

Successful bid

There are two more items to think about: how to get the car home; and insurance. If you can't drive it, your own or a hired trailer is one way, another is to have it shipped using the facilities of a local company. The auction house will also have details of companies specialising in the transport of cars.

Insurance for immediate cover can usually be purchased on site, but it may be more cost-effective to make arrangements with your own insurance company in advance, and then call to confirm the full details.

eBay & other online auctions?

eBay & other online auctions could land you a TR7 or TR 8 at a bargain price, though you'd be foolhardy to bid without examining it first, something most vendors encourage. A useful feature of eBay is that the geographical location of the car is shown, so you can narrow your choices to those within a realistic radius of home. Be prepared to be outbid in the last few moments of the auction. Remember, your bid is binding, and it will be very, very difficult to get restitution in the case of a crooked vendor fleecing you ... caveat emptor!

Be aware that some cars offered for sale in online auctions are 'ghost' machines. Don't part with any cash without being sure that the vehicle does actually exist, and is as described (usually pre-bidding inspection is possible).

11 Paperwork
– correct documentation is essential!

The paper trail
Classic, collector and prestige cars usually come with a large portfolio of paperwork, accumulated and passed on by a succession of proud owners. This documentation represents the real history of the car and from it can be deduced the level of care the car has received, how much it's been used, which specialists have worked on it, and the dates of major repairs and restorations. All of this information will be priceless to you as the new owner, so be very wary of cars with little paperwork to support their claimed history.

Registration documents
All countries/states have some form of registration for private vehicles, whether it's like the American 'pink slip' system or the British 'log book' system.

It is essential to check that the registration document is genuine, that it relates to the car in question, and that all the vehicle's details are correctly recorded, including chassis/VIN and engine numbers (if these are shown). If you are buying from the previous owner, his or her name and address will be recorded in the document: this will not be the case if you are buying from a dealer.

In the UK the current (EU-aligned) registration document is named V5C, and is printed in coloured sections of blue, green and pink. The blue section relates to the car specification, the green section has details of the new owner and the pink section is sent to the DVLA in the UK when the car is sold. A small section in yellow deals with selling the car within the motor trade.

In the UK the DVLA will provide details of earlier keepers of the vehicle upon payment of a small fee, and much can be learned in this way.

If the car has a foreign registration there may be expensive and time-consuming formalities to complete. Do you really want the hassle?

Roadworthiness certificate
Most country/state administrations require that vehicles are regularly tested to prove they are safe to use on the public highway and do not produce excessive emissions. In the UK that test (the MoT) is carried out at approved testing stations, for a fee. In the US the requirement varies, but most states insist on an emissions test every two years as a minimum, while the police are charged with pulling over unsafe-looking vehicles.

In the UK the test is required on an annual basis once a vehicle becomes three years old. Of particular relevance for older cars is that the certificate issued includes the mileage reading recorded at the test date and, therefore, becomes an independent record of that car's history. Ask the seller if previous certificates are available. Without an MoT the vehicle should be trailered to its new home, unless you insist that a valid MoT is part of the deal. (Not such a bad idea, this, as at least you will know the car was roadworthy on the day it was tested and you don't need to wait for the old certificate to expire before having the test done.)

Road licence

The administration of every country/state charges some kind of tax for the use of its road system, the actual form of the 'road licence,' and how it is displayed, varying enormously country-to-country and state-to-state.

Whatever the form of the 'road licence,' it must relate to the vehicle carrying it and must be present and valid if the car is to be driven legally on the public highway. The value of the license will depend on the length of time it will be valid.

In the UK if a car is untaxed because it has not been used for a period of time, the owner has to inform the licencing authorities, otherwise the vehicle's date-related registration number will be lost and there will be a painful amount of paperwork to get it re-registered.

Certificates of authenticity

For many makes of collectible car it is possible to get a certificate proving the age and authenticity (e.g. engine and chassis numbers, paint colour and trim) of a particular vehicle; these are sometimes called 'Heritage certificates' and if the car comes with one it is a definite bonus. If you want to obtain a certificate, the relevant owners club is the best starting point.

If the car has been used in European classic car rallies it may have a FIVA (Federation Internationale des Vehicules Anciens) certificate. The so-called 'FIVA Passport,' or 'FIVA Vehicle Identity Card,' enables organisers and participants to recognise whether or not a particular vehicle is suitable for individual events. If you want to obtain such a certificate go to www.fbhvc.co.uk or www.fiva.org. There will be similar organisations in other countries, too.

Valuation certificate

Hopefully, the vendor will have a recent valuation certificate, or letter signed by a recognised expert, stating how much he, or she, believes the particular car to be worth (such documents, together with photos, are usually needed to get 'agreed value' insurance). Generally, such documents should act only as confirmation of your own assessment of the car rather than a guarantee of value as the expert has probably not seen the car in the flesh. The easiest way to find out how to obtain a formal valuation is to contact one of the specialist suppliers listed in Chapter 16.

Service history

Often these cars will have been serviced at home by enthusiastic (and hopefully capable) owners for a good number of years. Nevertheless, try to obtain as much service history and other paperwork pertaining to the car as you can. Naturally, dealer stamps, or specialist garage receipts, score most points in the value stakes. However, anything helps in the great authenticity game, items like the original bill of sale, handbook, parts invoices, and repair bills all adding to the story and character of the car. Even a brochure correct to the year of the car's manufacture is a useful document and something that you could well have to search hard to locate in future years. If the seller claims that the car has been restored, then expect receipts and other evidence from a specialist restorer.

If the seller claims to have carried out regular servicing, ask what work was completed, when, and seek some evidence of it being done. Your assessment of the car's overall condition should tell you whether the seller's claims are genuine.

12 What's it worth to you?

– let your head rule your heart!

Condition

If the car you've been looking for is a really cheap 'for restoration' model then you've probably not bothered to use the marking system in Chapter 9 (Serious Evaluation) and may not have even got as far as using that chapter at all. However, do take a look at Chapter 13 (Do you really want to restore?) before buying! If you did use the marking system in Chapter 9, you'll know whether the car is in Excellent (maybe Concours), Good, Average or Poor condition or, perhaps, somewhere in-between these categories. This information should enable you to use at least a couple of the many classic/collector car magazines that run regular price guides. As with any classic car the extent and quality of any restoration work and, particularly with TR7s, upgrade work has a marked effect on the cars resale value and this can often make it difficult to equate one car with the next.

Trends can change, too. The values published in the magazines vary from one magazine to another, as do their scales of condition, so read carefully the guidance notes they provide and use more than one magazine's assessments. Use the internet to help gauge asking prices and the auction houses to assess what a comparable car actually sells for. Bear in mind that a car that is truly a recent show winner, or one that has very low mileage and never been restored, could be worth more than the highest scale published to someone who is looking for these specifics. However, maybe the asking price(s) is in the vendor's head, making it helpful to establish how long his/her car has been on the market. Some websites obligingly show when the advert was first placed.

Since most buyers will not be prepared to pay for a car in show/concours condition, relate the level of condition that you judge the car to be in with the appropriate guide price. How does the figure compare with the asking price? Before you start haggling with the seller, consider what effect any variations/improvements from standard specification might have on the car's value. If you are buying from a dealer, remember there will be a dealer's premium on the price but some warranty benefits, too.

Desirable options/extras

Drop-head variants
5-speed gearbox
Up-rated suspension all-round with firmer springs and polyurethane front and rear suspension bushes
Upgraded front and rear suspension telescopic inserts (front) and dampers (rear)
Upgraded brakes
Larger diameter wheels
Electric fan conversion
Electronic ignition conversion
Tubular exhaust manifolds and sports exhaust system
Mohair Hood
Sprint engine (with compatible ancillaries) conversion
Good V8 conversions
Uprated 'Hi Torque' starter motor, particularly on V8 conversions

Undesirable features

Non-original colour
Fibreglass body panels

The principal reason for enlarging the wheel diameter is to increase the space available for the front brakes, but the upgrade also gives owners the opportunity to fit larger width rims and, thus, larger cross-section tyres (particularly beneficial on powerful V8 conversions) and, if they wish, to fit different pattern wheel centres.

Modern 'Hi Torque' starter motors are more powerful, lighter, and draw less battery current than the original units.

Striking a deal

Negotiate on the basis of your condition assessment, mileage, and fault rectification cost. Also take into account the car's specification. Be realistic about the value, but don't be completely intractable: a small compromise on the part of the vendor or buyer will often facilitate a deal at little real cost.

13 Do you really want to restore?
– it'll take longer and cost more than you think ...

While the mechanics of the TR7 range are not daunting, it's the bodyshell that presents the main restoration challenge for most of us and brings me to recommend you buy a restored car, and a recently restored car at that. Only consider restoration if the car has special meaning for you (your dad's car perhaps) or is a genuine TR8, Sprint or Spider. Restoration usually makes no financial sense whatsoever.

The restoration of a bodyshell is not, panel-by-panel, actually terribly difficult and there is help available (see 'Books' in Chapter 16); it's just the sheer volume of work required and the time that it will take at home that is daunting. Even in a professional body shop the work takes a long time and the consequential cost makes this solution impractical for the vast majority. At one time, one could purchase relatively rust-free re-imported bodyshells that dramatically reduced the restoration work required and allowed a fairly swift home (or professional) body restoration, but, although you may still be lucky, those shells have largely been snapped up. Therefore, at first sight, the solution is straightforward: buy a brand-new bodyshell, get it painted, and start the mechanical restoration and re-assembly at home. However, before you get excited, please cast your eyes back to Chapter 2 generally, and the cost of a new bodyshell in particular. Add in the cost of painting and budget for the required mechanical, electrical, and trim work, then check your total with the highest re-sale value you can find and draw your own conclusions as to the financial sense of a restoration exercise. You will almost certainly conclude that there is more financial sense in finding and purchasing an already well-restored car, even if the search is a long one.

It is a sad but inescapable fact that all too frequently the owner fails to complete his restoration project. Often, the incomplete car then forms the basis for an 'abandoned-project' entry in the 'For Sale' columns, the owner rarely recovering his costs.

One reason for many home restorations stopping short of completion is that the owner underestimates the technical issues, the volume of work, or the timescale involved. The technical, cost, and time issues are largely trade-offs. The more technically competent you are, the more you can do yourself. The more you can do yourself, the less the project should cost but the longer it will take. Bearing this circle in mind, you need to ask yourself whether you have the finances to seek professional help if, and when, needed. Probably the single most frequent reason for incomplete restoration projects is that the costs proved more than was initially envisaged, followed fairly closely by the work taking far longer than was expected. Even for the experienced, the costs and the time-scales are *always* more than was expected!

Even before you buy a 'restoration project' car, prepare for and plan the restoration very carefully. Most people only carry out one restoration in their lives so look through Chapter 16 and seek advice from club members who have done it, read the relevant books, and talk to the professionals before you start. Where something can be postponed for a year or two (eg perhaps an engine rebuild), plan to do so. Where you have to get the whole job done thoroughly first time (eg body panel repairs and paint spraying), be sure you do so, even if it necessitates using professionals with that part of the project. You will have seen some examples in earlier chapters of extensive corrosion, but here are a few extra shots to re-emphasise what you'd be getting into and the fact that the bodyshell corrosion always goes further than it first appears.

At the rear of the bodyshell there are the wheelarches to consider. Corrosion to this degree will not only necessitate new metal shaping for, and welding to, the inner and outer wheelarch, but almost certainly signal rotten suspension mountings, rear sills, and, of course, major weaknesses in the main structural sill/rockers ...

... which never fails to surprise at the volume of corroded, in this case eaten-away, metal revealed. This was the extra DHC stiffening member at the rear of each sill, which is now providing no structural rigidity whatsoever.

At the front, this is what the first step will likely reveal ...

... while it does not take long to progress to here – a new turret. However, note the corrosion in the rest of the wheelarch, suggesting that the cutting-away of corroded metal has merely paused while some reference points are still in situ.

If the engine, clutch, and gearbox are OK, then do not refurbish them for the sake of it. Nevertheless, do you have the facilities at home to take the assembly out if/when you have to ...

... and the skill to strip and re-assemble the front struts with new damper inserts?

Paint faults generally occur due to lack of protection/maintenance, or poor preparation prior to a respray or touch-up. Some of the following conditions may be present in the car you're looking at:

Orange peel

This appears as an uneven paint surface, similar in appearance to the skin of an orange, hence the name. The fault is caused by the failure of atomized paint droplets to flow into each other when they hit the surface. It's sometimes possible to erase the effect with proprietary paint cutting/rubbing compound or very fine grades of abrasive paper. A respray may be necessary in severe cases. Consult a bodywork repairer/paint shop for advice on the particular car.

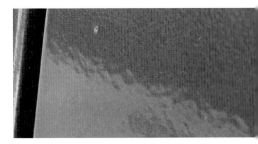

Orange peel.

Cracking

Severe cases are likely to have been caused by too heavy an application of paint (or filler beneath the paint). Also, insufficient stirring of the paint before application can result in components being improperly mixed, and cracking can result. Incompatibility with the paint already on the panel can have a similar effect. To rectify the problem it's necessary to rub down to a smooth, sound finish before respraying the affected area.

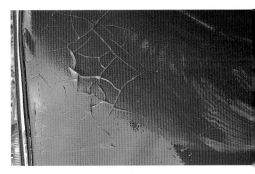

Cracking.

Crazing

Sometimes the paint takes on a crazed rather than a cracked appearance when the problems mentioned under 'Cracking' are present. This problem can also be caused by a reaction between the underlying surface and the paint. Paint removal and respraying the problem area is usually the only solution.

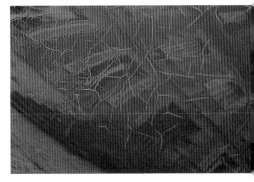

Crazing.

Blistering

Almost always caused by corrosion of the metal beneath the paint. Usually perforation will be found in the metal and the damage will be worse than that suggested by the area of blistering. The metal will have to be repaired before repainting.

Micro blistering

Usually the result of an economy respray where inadequate heating has allowed moisture to settle on the car before spraying. Consult a paint specialist, but usually damaged paint will have to be removed before partial or full respraying. Can also be caused by car covers that don't 'breathe.'

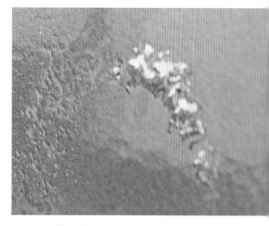

Reaction and rust blistering.

Fading

Some colours, especially reds, are prone to fading if subjected to strong sunlight for long periods without the benefit of polish protection. Sometimes proprietary paint restorers and/or paint cutting/rubbing compounds will retrieve the situation. Often a respray is the only real solution.

Peeling

Often a problem with metallic paintwork when the sealing lacquer becomes damaged and

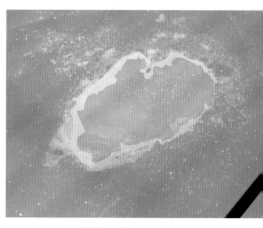

Peeling lacquer.

begins to peel off. Poorly applied paint may also peel. The remedy is to strip and start again!

Dimples

Dimples in the paintwork are caused by polish residue (particularly silicone types) not being properly removed before respraying. Paint removal and repainting is the only solution.

Dents

Small dents are usually easily cured by the 'Dentmaster,' or equivalent process, that sucks or pushes out the dent (as long as the paint surface is still intact). Companies offering dent removal services usually come to your home: consult your telephone directory.

15 Problems due to lack of use
– just like their owners, TR7s & TR8s need exercise!

When you are looking at potential purchases bear in mind that, after long periods of inactivity, even in the best of conditions, the following problems are likely depending upon the period of inactivity, storage conditions, pre-storage preparation, and whether any intermittent exercise (see below) has taken place:

Even in covered but outside shed/carport conditions, deterioration can be very marked throughout the car, but no more so than in alloy components. Seized pistons are obviously not on view here, but note that the TR7's cylinder head presents major problems when it becomes necessary to remove it to repair the engine. The slant configuration prevents oil from covering the studs, and the dissimilar metals (steel/aluminium) encourages corrosion, apparently 'welding' the head to the block and adding to the difficulty of restoring this engine.

• Pistons can seize in the engine's cylinders due to corrosion.
• Pistons can corrode in the carburetor dashpot(s).
• Pistons in brake and clutch calipers, and slave and master cylinders can seize.
• The bonnet/hood cable and catch can seize/freeze.
• The clutch may seize if the plate becomes stuck to the flywheel because of corrosion.
• Lip seals in the main working components stick to their respective shafts and can be damaged upon starting.
• Brake fluid absorbs water from the atmosphere and should be renewed every two years in any event.
• However, in storage old fluid with a high water content can cause corrosion within the braking system and pistons/calipers to seize/freeze. This in turn can cause brake failure when the water turns to vapour near hot braking components.
• With lack of use, the shock-absorbers/dampers will lose their elasticity or even seize. Creaking, groaning, and stiff suspension are signs of this problem.
• Radiator hoses may have perished and split, possibly resulting in the loss of all coolant. Window and door seals can harden and leak. Gaitors/boots can crack. Wiper blades will harden.
• The battery will be of little use if it has not been charged for many months. Earthing/grounding problems are common when the connections have corroded. Old bullet- and spade-type electrical connectors commonly rust/corrode and will need disconnecting, cleaning, and protection (eg Vaseline). Sparkplug electrodes will often have corroded in an unused engine. Wiring insulation can harden and fail.
• Fuel will loose its volatility and the tank will be best emptied and refilled. If water is sitting in the bottom of the tank, the tank will likely corrode and the fuel carry rust particles into the induction system.

• Mild steel exhaust systems corrode when a car is unused as the result of the high water content and combustion gasses trapped in the system. Thus, expect non-stainless systems to have to be replaced as a matter of course as part of your re-commissioning costs.

You will minimize your car's degeneration during storage if you start and run as much of the car as possible for 15 to 20 minutes once per month. This is particularly valuable if you have the wheels, particularly the rears, safely up on axle stands and can thus exercise the clutch, gearbox, rear axle, and brakes. Ensure the engine is used for long enough to open the thermostat whereupon you should circulate the coolant with some vigour (i.e. do not leave the car idling) for a minimum of five minutes. I personally like 2500rpm for these warm-ups. After which check and pump-up the tyres to running pressures and rotate the wheels, particularly if they are still on the ground. Disconnect the earth/ground terminal from the battery until it comes time for another start-up and connect a battery conditioner or trickle charger for a few hours before the car's next exercise period.

Furthermore, never leave the car unused for any extended periods with:
• The hand/parking brake 'on' as the shoes can rust to the drums and the cable seize/freeze.
• The weight of the car on the tyres. An unchanged position develops flat spots, resulting in (sometimes-temporary) vibration. Furthermore, the tyre walls may crack or develop blister-type bulges, necessitating new tyres.
• Weak or no anti-freeze protection in the coolant. The corrosion inhibitors in anti-freeze help prevent corroded internal waterways and, of course, also stop freezing which can cause core plugs to be pushed out and even cracks in the block or head. Silt settling and solidifying can cause subsequent overheating.
• Old/well-used engine oil in the sump/oil-pan – the acid that builds up during combustion corrodes bearings.

One would think that the condition of the seat generally, and the foam seat cushions in particular, was dependent solely upon usage. However, seats – indeed, all trim – respond badly to prolonged storage unless in the most favourable of conditions. The foam cushions actually turn to powder with time, whether or not in use.

16 The Community
– key people, organisations and companies in the TR7/TR8 world

Clubs

Triumph Sports Owners Association (Victoria)
PO Box 5020, GPO Melbourne,
Victoria 3001, Australia
www.tsoavic.com

Triumph Wedge Owner Association
(Formally TR8 Car Club of America)
www.triumphwedgeowners.org

TR Drivers Club
12 Puxton Drive, Kidderminster, Worc,
DY11 5DR, England
Tel 01562 825000
www.trdrivers.com

TR Register
1B Hawksworth, Southmead Industrial
Park, Didcot Oxon, OX11 7HR,
England
Tel 01235 818866
www.tr-register.co.uk

Vintage Triumph Register
PO Box 655, Howell, MI 48844, US
www.vtr.org

World Wide TR7 TR8 Club
NFD, PO Box 76, Leeds, LS25 9AG,
England
Tel 01977 681949
www.tr7-tr8.com

UK main restorers, repairers, dealers and spares suppliers

Brian Kitley Triumphs (Sprint
Specialist)
Somerset, England
Tel 07704 457168n
www.briankitleytriumphs.co.uk

James Paddock
6 Chantry Ct, Chester West Park,
Chester, CH1 4QN, England
Tel 01244 399899
www.jamespaddock.co.uk

Rimmer Bros
Sleaford Road, Bracebridge Heath,
Lincoln, LN4 2NA, England
Tel 01522 568000
www.rimmerbros.co.uk

Robsport International
Units 1-3 North End, Dunsbridge
Turnpike, Shepreth, Nr Royston, SG8
6RA, England
Tel 01763 262263
www.robsport.co.uk

S+S Preparations
Glen Mill Classic Car Centre,
Newchurch Road, Stacksteads, Bacup,
Lancs, OL13 0NH, England
Tel 01706 874874
www.ss-preparations.co.uk

US main specialist spares suppliers

Roadster Factory, The
PO Box 332, Killen Road, Armagh,
PA 15920, US
Tel (800)678-8764
www.the-roadster-factory.com

TS Imported Automotive
108 Jefferson Street, Pandora, OH
45877, US
Tel (419) 384-3022
www.tsimportedautomotive.com

Victoria British Ltd
PO Box 14991, Lenexa,
KS 66285-4991, US
Tel (800) 255-0088
www.longmotor.com

Wedgeparts
Nashville, Tennessee, US
Evening Tel (931) 801 0509
www.wedgeparts.com

Wedge Shop, The
111 Dean Street, Taunton,
MA 02780, US
Tel (508) 880-5448
www.thewedgeshop.com

Gearbox rebuilding
First Gear
3 Church View, Beckingham, Doncaster,
DN10 4PD, England
Tel 01427 848101

Brakes specialists
EBC
EBC Buildings, Countess Road,
Northampton, NN5 7EA, England
Tel 01604 583344
or; 806 Buchanan Blvd, Unit 115-256,
Boulder City, Las Vegas, NV89005, US

Hi Spec Motorsport
Unit 5 Parker Ind Centre, Watling St,

Dartford, Kent, DA2 6EP, England
Tel 01322 286850
www.hispecmotorsport.co.uk

Rally Design
Units 8-10, Upper Brents Ind Est,
Faversham, Kent, ME13 7DZ, England
Tel 01795 531871
www.rallydesign.co.uk

Books
TR7: The Untold Story
by David Knowles,
ISBN: 978-1-861268-91-4
How to Restore Triumph TR7/8
by Roger Williams,
ISBN: 1-904788-24-6
How to Improve Triumph TR7/8
by Roger Williams,
ISBN: 1-903706-68-8
Original Triumph TR7 and TR8
by Bill Piggott,
ISBN: 0-7603-0972-8
The Complete Guide to TR7 and TR8
by William Kimberly,
ISBN: 090-1564-532

All the TR7/8 focused clubs run numerous meeting and events throughout each year, bringing the Wedge community together. This is a typical meeting in the UK where like-minded enthusiasts meet for socialising, fun, and some friendly competition. Meetings also occur in various quarters of the UK, and there is much club activity in the US too, so joining one (or more) of the clubs not only has technical but social benefits as well. Meetings take various formats, including driving, static, concours, and spares days, and often a combination of them. The TR Register/World Wide TR7/8s National Meeting, to explore probably the biggest example, will take place over a weekend; attended by owners of all TR models, it involves 'run-outs,' concours, and other 'condition' competitions if you wish to enter and attracts a large number of trade and indeed private spares vendors. However, there are many smaller, but no less enjoyable, meetings, as well as countless local monthly informal/social gatherings throughout the country.

17 Vital statistics
– essential data at your fingertips

Common features
• Manufactured from September 1974 to October 1981, although the model was not announced until January 1975 in the US, and May 1976 in Europe.
• Initially the car was only offered as a Fixed-head Coupe (FHC), with the Drop-head Convertible (DHC) being introduced to the US from early 1979, and in Europe a year later.
• Electrics: 12-volt. Ignition via coil and distributor. Alternator.

4-cylinder TR7 details
Engine
Water-cooled 1998cc/122ci, iron block with single overhead 5-bearing camshaft running in an aluminium head. Block inclined at 45-degrees to left side. Bore 90.3mm, stroke 78.0mm. The engine number is in small letters/numbers located under number 2 and 3 cylinders on the higher/carburettor side of the engine.

Typically a two-letter prefix identifies the intended sales market (UK/European vehicles were identified by 'CG' while Canadian, Australian, Japanese, and North American vehicles were identified using 'CG' up to 1977 and 'CV' from 1977 onwards) and is followed by 5 numbers and a two-letter suffix (for example CG37607HE).

Carburetion
Twin 1.75in HS6 SU, twin 1.75in HIF6/waxstat SU, single Stromberg 1.75in CD150, twin Stromberg 1.75in CD150 carburettors or L-Jetronic multi-point Efi depending upon year and original market.

Gearbox
Early cars were fitted with 4-speed manual. Post the move to Canley all manual vehicles were fitted with a 5-speed gearbox and original such vehicles identified by the letter 'F' after the commission number (F= five-speed). TR7 automatics were fitted with a Borg Warner 65 3-speed autobox.

Brakes
Front 241mm (9.5in) diameter with 9.5mm (3/8in) width discs. Rear drums. Dual-line close-coupled servo operating on all four brakes. Handbrake operates on rear drums that vary with model (203mm/8in diameter, 38mm/1.5in on 4-speed and all automatic gearbox models, 228mm/9in diameter x 229mm/1.75in on 5-speed versions).

Battery location
Engine bay.

8-cylinder TR8 details
Production dates/chassis numbers
• For 1977/78 year cars made in Speke the TR8 FHC chassis number started 'ACN.'

• For Speke/Canley's 1978/79 year cars a TR8 FHC chassis number started 'TCN.'
• A TR8 DHC chassis number started 'TCV.'
• For Canley/Solihull's 1979/80/81 year cars check the 5th position that denotes engine fitted (eg. 'TPVDV8AT208267' where J=2-litre four-cylinder [TR7] and V=3.5-litre V8 [TR8]).
• For Solihull's 1981/2 year cars check the 7th position that denotes engine fitted. (eg. 'SATPV458XBA407609' where 1=2-litre four-cylinder [TR7] and 5=3.5-litre V8 [TR8]).

Engine
Water-cooled 3528cc/215ci, 8-cylinders in 90-degree V-configuration. Single camshaft running in an aluminium block with two aluminium cylinder heads. Bore 88.9mm, stroke 71mm. All TR8s were fitted with engines employing the following prefixes:
10E = Federal model (carburetor induction)
11E = Federal model auto transmission (carburetor induction)
12E = Californian model
13E = Californian model with auto transmission
14E = Efi model
15E = Efi model with auto transmission
20E = UK spec model (carburetor induction)

Carburetion
Twin 1.75in Stromberg CD150 carburettors or L-Jetronic multi-point Efi depending upon year and market (note: no genuine TR8 will be fitted with SU carburetors).

Gearbox
All manual vehicles had the 5-speed gearbox, while the Borg Warner 65 3-speed automatic was also offered which, behind a V8 engine, was quite acceptable and popular in US.

Brakes
Front 244mm (9.6in) diameter with 14.3mm (9/16in) width discs. Rear drums. Dual-line close-coupled servo operating on all four brakes. Handbrake operates on 9in diameter rear drums.

Battery location
Right side of boot/trunk.

Air-conditioning
Air-conditioning was an optional variation so may or may not be fitted. However, if it isn't fitted, check for the little door flaps that should be fitted in the footwells.

Power steering
Fitted to all but a very small number of TR8s.

Number of cars built per model
TR7 Drop-head Convertibles ...24,864
TR7 Fixed-head Coupes..........86,784

DHC Spiders ....1200-2000 (estimated)
DHC Sprints ....None
FHC Sprints............................50-60 (estimated, although the model was never
                                          officially launched as such and, consequently, it is
                                          likely that only a fraction of this number were
                                          sold)
TR8s ....20 for the UK market
                                          2570 for export
                                          2590 in total (but other contemporary sources
                                          suggest as many as 2815 were made. Although
                                          imprecise, these figures give you the order of, in
                                          automobile terms, the sadly small volumes produced)

Commission/VIN numbers

The TR7 was built in three different locations, each with a different Commission/VIN number:

• Production started at Speke in Liverpool using an 'ACG' prefix in 1974. Pre-production volumes 'staggered' through the summer and volume production started in November 1974. Speke No2 plant closed May 26th 1978 with TR7 commission number 'ACG44328.'

• Canley (near Coventry) produced its first car in October 1978, starting with commission number 'TCG100000' using bodyshells made by Pressed Steel Fisher.

• In 1980 Swindon took over bodyshell production and much of the pressings, although Speke No1 plant continued producing some pressings for a while

    However, main assembly moved to the Rover plant at Solihull using commission prefix 'TP.' Production continued there until the end of all TR production in October 1981. From March 31st to August 1980 the TR7 was produced concurrently at Canley and Solihull.

• The Sprint pre-production models were also a multi-factory product, albeit part built at Speke and shipped for finishing at the Engineering department at Canley. Canley used to have to substantially rework all Speke cars destined for Press trials and similar launches because the output from there, especially at the start of any new model, was so poor. All factory made Sprints were FHC models.

• The Sprint had a unique commission numbering sequence starting with 'ACH 1' to 'ACH 25,' then jumping to 'ACH 00501' to 'ACH 00536,' however, those original cars that do exist sort of 'escaped' in that the Sprint was never formally announced or officially sold. In fact, I understand British Leyland started writing the UK launch press release but found that the 0-60mph acceleration time was slower than the 8-valve car due, probably, to an overly high first gear ratio. Before anything could be resolved, the project was canned.

• The Spider variant was introduced into the US in late 1980 and built through 1981. Black paint, retro-reflective red 3M tape for exterior decals, and coach lines were used based upon an idea by Alan Edis and designed by Michelotti. Standard TR8-style alloy wheels were used, but with a brighter silver finish. Pewter-coloured extra-deep pile carpet was fitted, silver/grey trim (as used on some special versions of the MGB), air-con, AM/FM cassette radio, and 3-spoke sports steering wheel were all fitted to differentiate the model. The cars sold well, in spite a $1000 premium. Some 400 of the total made were in Californian Fuel-injected form.

The **Essential** Buyer's Guide™ series

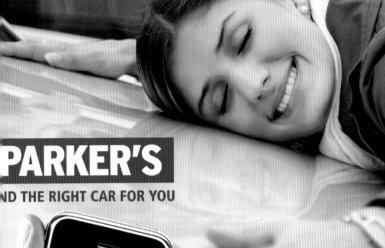

Index